# GARDENING FOR HEALTH AND NUTRITION

An Introduction to the Method
of Bio-Dynamic Gardening
Inaugurated by Rudolf Steiner

## John & Helen Philbrick

RUDOLF STEINER PUBLICATIONS
151 North Moison Road
Blauvelt, New York 10913, U.S.A.
1971

# Contents

# Introduction

I am supposed to speak about A CLOSER LOOK AT YOUR GARDEN, and I would like to have you imagine that you are a group of Garden Club people who know practically nothing about Bio-Dynamics. I want you to imagine that you are hearing about these things for the first time, hearing with a background of the kind of agriculture and knowledge of backyard gardening which the average person has. This was the kind of knowledge I had when we started in 1943 with a Victory Garden. My wife and I knew so little about gardening that we planted a row of potatoes for a windbreak!

I want you to go with me into the garden to see what we can observe that is there, and to see how to relate what we see to the total picture of the garden the year 'round.

When I step out into the garden, I go to meditate and commune with what's there. Every morning when the weather is decent, I get up at sunrise, take a mugfull of coffee and go into the garden just to look. You see, I am aware that God walked in the Garden in the cool of the day. Time and time again I find Him there. Often He opens my eyes to see things that I wouldn't otherwise see. From the outset I began to recognize that the most important things surrounding me in the garden are the Forces of Life. That life is the key to existence on this planet.

This becomes the focal point. Life is the thing that must be put in the center. As I look around my neighbors' gardens and talk with them I discover that they have no understanding of what this life is all about. This is partly because they have never seen it. They have never experienced it. One reason is that agriculture and even backyard gardening today, in the orthodox sense, is not based on life but is based on its opposite, death. The average farmer, when he goes into the field in the morning, is not going with a concept of life but with a concept of death. He goes out to get rid of things. He gets rid of the bugs, he gets rid of the weeds, he gets rid of the insects, he gets rid of the fungus. He gets rid of anything that gets in his way. This is his prime purpose in order that he may get for himself and make by his own efforts the things he wants most to grow. The only way he can do it is to try to kill things. The reason he can do this is because he doesn't know what life is all about. And the reason he doesn't realize is because life, or livingness, is something you cannot get hold of. You cannot capture it. You cannot take it into a laboratory. Nor can you put it under a microscope and look at it, measure it, or experience it with the senses which give us sight, smell, touch and hearing.

Now there is a perfectly good reason why he is this way. It is because his science has taught him these things. I believe one of the major problems of the scientific world today is that chemistry got started before biology. Chemistry in its earliest stages was a science of dead things. It is understandable why this happened, because men first worked in the scientific world. And men are much less sensitive to this thing we call life than are women. Women are the bearers of life. It's a part of their very being and they are infinitely more conscious of it than men are. Another reason is that men have an insatiable curiosity to take things apart to see what they're made of.

It is Christmas. It's just barely daybreak. Junior, about four years old, can't wait any longer to get downstairs and under the Christmas tree to see what is there. Under that tree are half a dozen mechanical toys, but I'll guarantee that before Christmas Day is over, at least one of those toys won't work any more. Why? Because Junior took it apart to see what made it go. Once it's taken apart, it doesn't work any more.

Now when Junior grows up, he still has this curiosity. He begins to take living things apart to study their structure and behavior. But when he is dealing with something that is alive, the minute he takes it apart it is no longer what it was when he started, because the life is gone. But he can't see this life. He can't weigh it. He can't measure it. He isn't really conscious that there is any difference. You have to become conscious of this life before you become aware how very important it is.

There are evidences of this life all around you. We used to have milk goats, and we also had cats. I would get up in the morning to find the cats crying for something to eat. I'd go to the icebox and get a little milk, put it down, and they would drink it. Then I would get the milk pail and go out to the barn. The minute I would come in from the barn, those cats were still ravenous and they had to have a bowl of that warm milk. If I had reversed the process, they would not touch the milk from the icebox because they could tell the difference. One was yesterday's milk. They really wanted today's milk. So even though they were full of yesterday's milk, they begged for today's milk because it tasted so much better. Reverse the process, and they were not interested.

You and I can learn to experience this factor of life. There have been two instances when I have felt it most keenly. One I feel every summer in June when, dressed in my bee-suit and bee-veil, I go into poor Mrs. So-and-so's orchard. She is so distraught. She wanted to hang the clothes out this morning but "There's a swarm of bees in the yard. Can't you please do something?" There they are, hanging from the limb in that beautiful shape. The empty hive is underneath, ready to receive them and I shake the branch. Immediately the air is absolutely alive with living things. It's the most exciting experience to stand there and realize that all around you are these insects just buzzing and buzzing with so much life. They are all full of honey and they are just flying very quietly. I think the greatest let-down I ever feel is when the last of them have settled down in the hive and the cover is on and it is time to go away and leave them. It's almost a depressing feeling in contrast to the wonderful exhilaration of this life experience.

The other one I experienced for the first time when I went to Ashfield in March of 1958. I stepped into a sugar-house which was in operation. There in the great stove was a tremendous roaring fire. The pine and hardwood in this great bed of ashes were roaring and flaming, and the life forces and life energies from the sun were rapidly released from the great burning logs. This fire was keeping the life-blood of the maple tree boiling rapidly in a long shallow tray. And the entire room was completely gray with live steam. Again I was aware of the fact that here is life, and how wonderful it is and how completely it fills one's being. This is a factor which motivates the world and the universe in which we live. So we have this force that we can begin to look for when we go out into the garden.

The kind of gardening I practice is Bio-Dynamics, and it has to do with the inter-relatedness (dynamics) of these life forces (bio). When you become aware of Biodynamics, you become aware that everything that is alive is dependent upon everything else that's alive and it's all a marvelous network of living things which are constantly changing. This is what's going on in your garden, and you need to recognize what some of these things are.

Bio-Dynamics is no different from group dynamics. And group dynamics is a branch of psychology which is becoming quite popular these days. Group dynamics is nothing more nor less than the interrelatedness of human personalities. It all started up in Bethel, Maine a few years ago when they decided to carry out an experiment to see how people react on each other. They took twelve total strangers and locked them in a room for a whole day, just to see what would happen. They didn't give them any program. They didn't tell them what to think about. They didn't tell them anything at all, except to say, "We're going to let you out at four o'clock. Now have fun." And what happened? Well, the noisy ones began to be noisy because they always had been. And the mousy ones continued to be mousy because they felt more comfortable that way. But by noontime the noisy ones had run down and that gave the mousy ones a chance. At the end of the day, instead of having twelve individual peoople, they had one group. This thing actually had worked. The interrelated life forces of individual personalities, each one of them a living ego in itself, worked together to create this single whole.

Now anybody who has been the president of an organization, especially one that meets once a week or once a month, can understand what ı'm talking about. Some days you get to the gathering and you try to conduct the meeting and everybody is determined to have his own way. The whole thing is at sixes and sevens. On the other hand, sometimes you come to a meeting, where something tragic has happened to one of the members. Part of the business of the meeting deals with what the club can do about this tragedy, and immediately you no longer have a collection of individuals. It has now become a single group, all working together to see what they can do to help somebody else.

In this field of group dynamics each of us has the same experience. When you come into a group of total strangers and somebody introduces you to several people, one person stands out when you meet him. There is something that jumps out of him and hits you, and jumps out of you and hits him, and you think, "Gee this is a wonderful experience! I'd like to know more about that person." Then you go down the line and meet several others who don't affect you one way or the other. Perhaps down toward the end of the line there is somebody about whom you think, "I don't like that person. I don't care if I never see him again!" These same interrelationships are at work in the garden, just as they are at work among people but with one difference. If you don't like your surroundings, you can go elsewhere, but the plants cannot move about in the garden. Sometimes you have a very special plant that you are very anxious to get to grow and be healthy, but whatever you do, it doesn't respond. Perhaps you'd better look around and see who the neighbors are. You might dig it up and put it in another place with another set of plants and see if this won't make a difference.

There's another way this dynamic effect works from the level of group dynamics. If you have a group of delinquent boys that are very difficult to handle and are heading for trouble, if you can get a young man with a strong, virile personality to come and work with these boys, by the sheer strength of his personality he lifts the weaker boys up to a level where they can become useful citizens. This is done through the dynamics of the human personality.

The same principle works in the garden. One of the places where it works most evidently is in your rose bed. Most people, and I daresay most of the people I talk to in garden clubs, spend more money and more energy dousing the rose bed with all kinds of indescribable poisons than anything else in the garden. The reason for this is that the rosebush is one of the oldest plants known to man and almost from the beginning of time, man has been hybridizing the rose. Now, if you go to a dog show and buy a highly-bred cocker spaniel puppy, I guarantee that you'll spend most of your time at the Vet's, not because the animal itself is sickly, but because it's so highly bred that if there is any disease near it, it just picks it up. This is what happens in your rose bed. The answer is that we must find a plant that is just as opposite and just as primitive as it can be to plant with the roses. In this particular instance, the plant is garlic. Immediately someone wants to know if the rose bush will smell like the garlic and I say, "No, and you'll never get a garlic that smells like a rose," because it's not this that transfers. You're not thinking on the right level, you see. You should be thinking about these intangible dynamic forces.

I remember once back in Duxbury we were looking for a root of stinging nettle. We were told that stinging nettle in the tomato patch would help to prevent the fungus diseases, because the formic acid working through the inter-action of the feeder roots is absorbed by the tomato plant, giving a plant that is resistant to rot . . . So we decided we'd try it. This meant going in search of stinging nettle while visiting a conference center. In a field we came upon a plant which looked like mint. I reached down and picked it and started to smell of it. It was not mint . . . but it was nettle! At the house I asked the woman in charge if I could have a root of stinging nettle. She said "What ever do you want that for?" "Because

vi

it's good in the garden," I replied. Then she said, "Don't bother to go down to the field. There's some in the hollyhock bed and you can have all you want. We can't get rid of it." We walked to the hollyhock bed and sure enough, there was this wonderful clump of stinging nettle. As we stood and looked, we realized that the hollyhocks on either side of that stinging nettle were 18 inches taller than all the rest of the hollyhocks in the bed. It was because of the dynamic effect of this neighboring plant which was right there. They had seen this for several years and it never registered. They didn't see what they were looking at!

This is part of our trouble. Years ago, before we had quite so much chemistry, and before the farmer got three feet off the ground on his tractor, he was able to recognize what was happening on his farm. He could see how some plants did better than others in combinations, and he was able to make use of these observations. He was conscious of this life force.

One year I proved it in my garden by planting string beans in the strawberry patch. In another part of the garden I planted another row of string beans alone. Four weeks later anyone would have thought the beans in the strawberry patch were planted six weeks before, and the ones by themselves only four weeks before. This was because of this dynamic effect of the two neighboring plants in the soil. In some strange way the dynamic effect worked.

Now I don't know why it works, and frankly I don't really care, so long as I know that it does work. I'm willing to try it and to work with it, and to use it.

When we work in the garden, then, we are aware of the life forces and the life factor, and I ask myself "Where does this life come from?" Remembering the wisteria up around the porch which gets inside and grows much more scrawny and straggly and gets lighter and lighter green because it's in the dark, I conclude that this life comes from the sun. This sun is the light of our world. But the Sun of Righteousness said, "I am the Light of the world." "In Him was Life and the Life was the Light of men. The Light shone in the darkness and the darkness comprehended it not." Can these two suns be related? Let us see. When we look at the sun over a period of time, we discover that it is never the same, but that it is moving in cycles, in very wonderful cycles, all the time through the periods of the year.

Remember when you were a child playing with a magnifying glass, you could focus the sun's rays, even until they would burn? Let us imagine a horizontal line right here representing the surface of the earth. Down below it, under the earth, the focal point of the sun is found deepest on December 23rd, the shortest day in the year. Gradually as the days grow longer, that point moves toward the surface of the earth until on the 21st of March, when the day and night are the same length, it arrives at the surface. Then it moves out into the air where plants are now growing, until on June 23rd, or the Summer Solstice, it reaches its highest point and begins to descend again. Slowly it moves downward until on September 21st it touches the surface again, and then moves beneath the surface, reaching its deepest position on December 23rd one year later.

When we investigate further we learn that at the vernal equinox in March and again at the autumnal equinox in September, the bacterial action in the soil is most active, and that it is least active in June and December, the former because it is too hot, and the latter because it is too cold for bacterial activity. When we stop to think about it, the active times come when we clean up our gardens and when we should be doing spring housecleaning. It would be wiser to let your garden soil alone during the end of June and the first part of July. And, of course, no one works in the garden at midwinter when (in our climate at least) the ground is frozen solid.

If you were members of a Sunday School class, I would retrace this sun cycle in this way: On December 23rd we have the shortest day in the year. December 24th is about the same length. December 25th is the first day on which there is a measurable amount more of light. This is the day in which we celebrate the coming of the Light of World, the birth of Christ.

When we move to the Spring equinox in March, we find that Easter is the Sunday nearest the full moon after March 21st. This is the time, in nature, when everything is working contrary to gravity. This is the time we celebrate the Resurrection of Christ.

Now let us move to the Summer Solstice, the 23rd of June. This is Midsummer Night's Eve, the day before the feast of the birth of John the Baptist on June 24th. John the Baptist says of himself in St. John's Gospel, "He must increase, but I must decrease."

When we get to the autumnal equinox, we find the nearest church festival is September 29th, the Feast of St. Michael and All Angels. Now we are told that nobody believes in angels any more. It isn't popular! But the fact is that in the Gospel, wherever you find a supernatural event like the Annunciation, the Baptism, the Transfiguration, the Resurrection or the Ascension, you always find that there were "two men in white apparel" or "Behold, the angel of the Lord came." They were realities then. They are realities now. And the function of Michael here is to stand opposite to the Resurrection to witness that despite the fact that in nature everything seems to be dying, if we can only wait long enough, everything will be changed and the light of the world will come back, and we will go through the cycle again. All of these things are interrelated, and they all work together in a marvelous way to provide the life forces in their proper balance in the earth.

This is wonderful to meditate about. It is wonderful to contemplate. But it's also fascinating to try to discover where this interrelatedness works, and where it doesn't work. I had a good example of this when Dr. Pfeiffer visited us in Roanridge, Missouri. We were living in a little house which had a front porch and a short garden walk running from it to the gate. Next to the gate was a peach tree, and in the trunk of the peach tree was a sore. Once there had been a borer in the tree, but the borer had long since gone. Still I could not rid the tree of the infection in its trunk. I said, "Dr. Pfeiffer, why can't I cure this tree?" He went over to it, got down and looked very carefully at the hole in the tree. Then he stood back and looked all around the tree. Next he stood back still further and began to look all around the landscape. Finally he turned to me and said, "The trouble with that tree is that fence post." In utter amazement I said, "How can that fence post affect the tree?" Then he explained: "See that shelf fungus on the side of the fence post?" I nodded. "The function of the fungus," he went on, "is to return that dead tree to topsoil, because the fence post is really a dead tree. Now," said he, "there's just enough dead material in the hole in the tree to keep the spores of the fungus alive. Either get rid of the fence post, or spray it with crankcase oil and get rid of the fungus, and you'll cure your tree." You see, all this time I had been looking at the tree, because I didn't know any better. After that I began to look around to see what other things might be related.

Once we had a row of broccoli in the middle of our garden. One of the heads completely filled the top of a tomato basket. Two thirds of the way down the row were two plants that were alive with aphids, and there wasn't an aphid anywhere else in the row. I said to myself, "This doesn't make sense." The average farmer or gardener would go out and say, "How can I get rid of those bugs?" Instead of taking that attitude I tried to figure out why they were there, and I thought, "What are you trying to tell me that I'm doing that's wrong?" I looked at the ground and the soil. Pretty soon I discovered that those two plants, when they were transplanted, had received serious injuries to the roots. Nature was trying to say to me, "You can eat this one and this one, and this one and those plants down there, but these two plants are not fit for man or beast, so we get rid of them." Now if this is the function of these sucking or biting insects, what does this tell us about our management of the fruit trees? In 1957 we visited the USDA and heard them advocating that every fruit tree should be sprayed 22 times. This was their only solution.

When people looked at my orchard out at Roanridge, that we had planted and raised and grown, with those beautiful great big peaches, I used to say, "If I should find it necessary to spray these trees, I would be spraying to destroy a measurable sized bug. What possible chance would the microlife in the soil have against the 40% of that poison that would land on the soil? The soil life would be killed. This tree would be living in a dying medium and the only way the tree can react to the dying soil is to change its cellular structure in the leaf itself. It becomes more cellulose, and this is what the bugs love. So next year we get a few more bugs, and I'd have to spray twice as much. Therefore I'd kill that much more in the soil and the tree would have to react that much more violently to a dying medium. This is the horrible cycle that we are in agriculturally with the management of our fruit trees. We do it because we don't really understand that these trees have to have insect life, and if they don't get it in the soil, they'll get it more and more in the top, and you're fighting a losing battle before you start. Here we should be dealing with life, not with death."

One day, after she had done some research, my wife handed me a chart on the distance that various feeder roots of common vegetables travel in the ground under any one plant. They vary all the way from two feet to eight feet in diameter, so you can imagine what happens in the soil.

Now the combination of soil bacteria under every family of plants is different, and the more mixed the culture is, the more opportunity the plants have of getting a "steak" dinner here a "fish" dinner here, a "vegetable" dinner here, and another kind of dinner here, so the health of this plant is well balanced. This again is something we should be aware of in relation to the life forces in the soil. The more we think about it and the more we consider it, the more we learn that we can look beneath the surface of what we see and discover something infinitely more wonderful that lies behind it.

One Sunday morning I was getting ready to preach a sermon and I didn't have an idea what to preach about. It isn't easy fifty-two Sundays in the year to be ready with something that's worth listening to. Well, this particular morning I was walking in the garden trying to figure out what I should say. I looked at all the different kinds of vegetables in front of me. There were beets and carrots which provide the wonderful root vegetables for us to eat. The Swiss chard and spinach provide a leaf vegetable. Cauliflower and broccoli provide an edible bud. Beans and peas and corn give us edible seed to eat. These gifts were all there waiting for me to use. But, as I looked further, I saw something even deeper than this. We grow the vegetables in raised beds, according to the Bio-Dynamic system — and at the end of each bed a different kind of herb is growing. All these herbs give us a multitude of flavors, even more subtle than flowers. There are many different kinds of tastes for many different purposes. Not only that, there was Saint Johnswort growing as a weed and also as an herb in the garden, and many other aromatic plants there, like the plantain and sourdock and others which provide medicine for our use. But the most mysterious thing is how all these different plants can grow in exactly the same soil. There are "diversities of gifts but the same spirit." There was my sermon!

Now we are able to look, not only at things we see with our outward eyes, but also at things we grasp with our inward spiritual life, because now our inner eyes have been opened. As we think about it, we remember that back when the Italian Primitives were painted, whenever a supernatural event was depicted, the lily was painted. This is because the lily has all food in the bulb. It is not dependent on the earth for anything, except rain, the moisture which comes from outside the earth. So the lily is a supernatural kind of plant. It speaks of Heaven. Now in those paintings we also find the opposite of this: Whenever a natural, earthly event is depicted, the rose is always found. This is because the rose is a plant which is of the earth, earthy. If you look at the rose bush, you see every thorn pointing toward the earth. Soon after the leaves have opened, they tend to go down toward the earth. Even the petals, after the rose begins to unfold, are drawn down toward the earth. If you have ever tried to dig up a rose bush, you know how the roots go way down deep and really hold in the soil. The early painters put those concepts into their paintings because they knew in their innermost selves that these are the plants, in the world in which we live, which tell us about these things in the spiritual world.

Now for what it's worth I'm going to tell you that I feel it is important for every Christian farmer or gardener to have at least a little patch of wheat as well as a grapevine on his place, because in the night in which He was betrayed, our Lord took bread, which is the essence of the wheat, and after supper He took the cup which contained the essence of the grape, and when we have both of these plants together, we have the Presence of the Light of the World, the Light which is the Life of Men.

Now the wheat is a monocotyledon, while the grape is a dicotyledon. That is, the wheat is a single-celled seed, and the veins in the leaf are parallel. The grape is a dicotyledon; it is formed in two halves. There is a central vein up the leaf, and the leaf is divided in halves. The wheat is an annual, while the grape is a perennial.

Both the grape and the wheat sacrifices its beauty for its usefulness. You hardly know when the wheat blooms, but we recall the golden grain waving in the wind. Similarly, nobody ever gathers grape blossoms to decorate a dining room table because they're so unimportant and stay hidden in the background. But if you look down on the wheat plant from above and see where the leaves grow off the stem, or if you observe the wheat while it is in bloom, you discover that intrinsically it takes the shape of a six-pointed star, that is, of the Star of David. If you cut a grape in half longitudinally, or if you count the points of the leaves, you find a five-pointed star, which is the shape of the Star the Wise Men followed. And in these two stars all of mankind is united in the wheat and grape, in the Body and Blood of the Savior of Mankind.

— Now go out and take a closer look at YOUR garden!

JOHN PHILBRICK

*March, 1962*

(The above is the substance of a lecture given at an Annual Summer Conference of the Bio-Dynamic Farming and Gardening Association)

# The Bio-Dynamic Gardener

To the casual observer it may appear that the Bio-Dynamic gardener or farmer goes to a great deal of extra work to produce his crops. This booklet is an attempt to explain what the Bio-Dynamic gardener is looking for and how he can succeed in producing food of very highest quality in an age when all our soils show the deteriorating effects of erosion, depletion, and fallout.

The Bio-Dynamic gardener watches for special factors. One of these is Balance. He tries to establish a balance between plants that deplete the soil and legumes which restore soil nitrogen. Already depleted soil he tries to balance with specially built composts to restore the soil fertility. In the building of this compost he uses certain preparations to activate the decomposing material and to enable it to draw in from the atmosphere substances which the crops will use. Finally, he is constantly aware of balances between forces in nature: heat and cold, night and day, summer and winter, and the effects of these forces on his soil and crops.

The Bio-Dynamic worker also concerns himself with a study of processes, whether he operates a large farm, a small homestead, or a tiny backyard garden. He observes and encourages the process of up-building, of growth. He is equally attentive to the process of decomposition, which breaks down substances and prepares them to return to topsoil. He watches his plants grow and flower and produce seed: but he also pays equal attention to plant substances decaying and falling into the earth to return as sprouting seed the following season.

It has been stated over and over again that Bio-Dynamics is not a collection of recipes, or favorite tricks to make things grow. There is only one general rule and that is that each plot of ground is different from every other plot and must be studied carefully and handled as an individual entity. Because of this individuality, it is impossible to lay down hard and fast rules, to say exactly what you must do or avoid doing. You have the opportunity to study and apply the following principles in complete freedom in your own garden.

If we were to tell you what to do, this would limit your own freedom. But we can recount the personal experiences we have had which have worked well for us, both in the production of adequate supplies of edible fruits and vegetables (about 60% of the total amount of foodstuffs we use in a year) and also in the maintenance of a high standard of personal health throughout the years. These are facts which cannot be set aside, and we give full credit to our conscientious practice of the system of Bio-Dynamic backyard gardening.

From our own experience we have worked out certain short-cuts and time savers which have made it relatively simple and economical to raise our own food while carrying on very busy lives at the same time. In these days when more and more people are demanding organically grown garden produce, it is noticeable that there are more consumers than producers. For many people the only way to get fresh, inexpensive garden produce is to grow it themselves. It is our concern to present gardening with Bio-Dynamics as simple, down to earth processes for producing one's own unsprayed organically grown vegetables with a minimum of time and labor and a maximum of enjoyment and deep satisfaction in the observation of and co-operation with nature.

The Bio-Dynamic farming and gardening method has grown and developed since 1922, on a foundation of advice and instruction given by Rudolf Steiner (1861-1925), an Austrian philosopher and educator.

The name "Bio-Dynamic" refers to a "working with the energies which create and maintain life." The term derives from two Greek words "bios" (life) and "dynamis" (energy). The use of the word "method" indicates that one is not dealing merely with the production of another fertilizer, organic though it is, but rather that certain principles are involved, which in their practical application secure a healthy soil and healthy plants — and which in turn produce healthful food for man and animals.

Briefly, the aims of the Bio-Dynamic method are:

1. To restore to the soil the organic matter which it needs to hold its fertility.

2. To restore to the soil a balanced system of functions.

A living soil includes not only chemicals, mineral and organic, but also a microlife, and conditions which encourage this invisible microlife in the topsoil.

3. To sponsor the most skillful use of organic matter as the basic factor for soil life. If organic manner is skillfully used, the garden gets the most out of the mineral constituents of the soil; nitrogen, phosphate, potash, lime, magnesium and the trace minerals. However, the organic matter is composted and completely digested and made available by the use of either the Bio-Dynamic preparations or of BD Compost Starter which was perfected by the late Dr. E. E. Pfeiffer and is still being manufactured according to his formula.

4. To further the skillful application of all the factors contributing to soil life and health; light and warmth, mineral elements, protein, carbohydrates, cellulose, starch all of which derive from the air (carbon dioxide, nitrogen, oxygen) and water.

5. To balance the interaction of substance and energy in soil and growing plant. When the soil is balanced, a healthy plant will grow and transmit both substance and energy as food for animal or man.

6. To include in the Bio-Dynamic way of treating manure and composts, a knowledge of enzymes, hormones and growth factors, as well as a knowledge of minerals and trace elements.

7. To restore and maintain the balance in a soil through proper crop rotation, cover crops and green manuring.

8. To recognize the importance of the entire environment of a farm or a garden. Therefore the restoration of the most beneficial environmental conditions (forests, wind-protection, water regulation) has been an important aim of the Bio-Dynamic method from its earliest years.

9. To realize that the soil has not only a chemical-mineral organic system, but also a physical structure. The maintenance of a crumbly, friable, deep, well-aerated structure is an absolute must if one wants to have a fertile soil. The Bio-Dynamic method is very specific about the proper cultivation of the soil in order to avoid structural damage. Many a farmer, even among the organic farmers, has defeated his aim by ruining the soil structure through unskillful cultivation.

# Planning the Vegetable Garden

Probably no subject has so many different approaches as a vegetable garden. Ask ten gardeners how to plant potatoes and you will get ten different answers. Even language idioms differ. People in some localities "put their seeds in" others, "put their garden out." Regardless of systems or opinions, the important thing is to make your own plan and follow it, to get the seeds out of their envelopes and into the earth where they will make productive returns.

## Make Garden Plans on Paper

Year after year we make our garden too large. The saying is old and threadbare perhaps, but it is worth keeping in mind: "Never plow up more space than your wife can take care of." Planning the garden on paper during the preceding winter makes it possible to scratch and erase and re-arrange until the right rows are in the right places. But even on paper, keep your garden small enough so that you can take good care of it. Even a small area can produce a large crop if it is well managed.

There are a number of simple, definite rules which experienced gardeners follow every year:

1. Keep the garden plan on a clipboard where it will be accessible but will not blow away in the wind on planting day.

2. Keep records of varieties, dates, plantings and any special treatment each year for reference the following year.

3. Locate the garden where the sun shines full on the ground during most of the day. Sunshine is requisite for all plants and they will thrive or not in proportion to the amount of sunshine they receive. It is possible to determine exactly where the shadows from neighboring trees will fall by finding out the degree of latitude of your state and figuring the length of the shadows when the sun is shining at that angle, in both winter and summer. Rows for planting are usually made from north to south, so the sun shines on the entire row from early morning to late afternoon.

The garden should be as near to the kitchen door as possible. This makes it easier to get out into the garden for weeding and cultivation. Many people like to walk in their garden (with a cup of coffee!) early in the morning, not to do any work, but just to absorb the freshness, to enjoy the coolness and to observe what changes in the growth and development of the plants have taken place during the night. A few minutes of quiet study in the garden in the cool of the day rewards the observer with heightened insight into the whole world of nature.

Much hard work can be avoided if the garden is placed near a supply of water, possibly piped by hose from the house. In the absence of a sillcock and hose, a rain barrel may be used, and rain water is especially good for plants. The compost heap should also be within easy carrying distance of the garden and water supply.

Tree roots take food from the soil in a circle which stretches as far from the trunk as the farthest branches. Within that circumference most garden plants will not flourish. Trees south of a garden will also cast a shade over the garden in early and late summer. While it is pleasant to work in the shade, the plants in the garden will suffer from lack of sunlight. Therefore, the garden should be located beyond the farthest reach of tree roots and beyond the shadows cast by trees south and west of the garden spot.

## Plant Where Weeds Flourish

If there is a good stand of weeds on the proposed garden spot, a garden should also grow well there. The weeds have been replenishing the soil with whatever was lacking in preparation for the next year's production. In other words, that area has been lying fallow, a practice which used to be a regular part of every crop rotation. If weeds will not grow on a given area, a vegetable garden will not do well there either.

Neither weeds, vegetables, nor grass will grow where the soil has been deeply burned. If there are signs of an old bonfire on your land, avoid planting there until you have had several years to rebuild fertility into the sterilized soil.

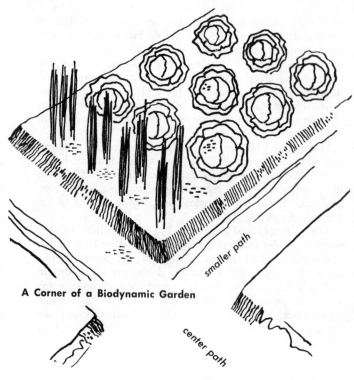

**A Corner of a Biodynamic Garden**

smaller path

center path

Figure 1.

### The Size of Your Garden

The size of the garden depends entirely on the needs of the family. With power tools or a garden tractor one can sow and care for a large area. The opposite extreme in size might be like the plot 25 by 51 feet called "A Weekend Vegetable Garden" grown by an experienced gardener who devoted 26 working hours during weekends over an entire season. Another similar garden plan is described and illustrated in Paul Dempsey's GROW YOUR OWN VEGETABLES. He calls this "the twenty minutes a day garden from April through November." The illustrations and explanations in this book make it worthwhile to study because it could save so much time and effort for the amateur gardener. Some seed companies get out small brochures telling how easy and quick it is to grow a luxuriant backyard garden, but some of these may call for a grain of salt!

Once you start a garden, you will quickly learn whether it is too large to care for, too small to produce enough food for your family's needs, or whether it is just right. Keeping records this year will help you to make plans for next year.

## The Typical Bio-Dynamic Garden: Raised Beds

The typical biodynamic vegetable garden is arranged in raised beds, one or several carefully chosen vegetables to a bed, with paths in the spaces between the beds. This makes a charming pattern with rectangular patches of various plants bordered by narrow paths. A convenient size for the beds is about fifteen feet long and about three and one half feet wide. They need not be raised more than four to five inches high. If herbs are planted at the ends of the raised beds, bordering the central path, the visitor walking down that path enjoys one herb after another. This is also an ideal arrangement when one runs along the path, gathering the ingredients for a salad at the last minute before dinner is served.

The wide beds with narrow paths between insure maximum use of the garden space, instead of wasting large areas in unproductive paths which must be kept weeded. The presence of plenty of paths also makes it possible in a short time to walk from any point in the garden to any other point, or to cut through the garden quickly to answer the telephone. Another advantage to this garden plan is that once the beds are laid out carefully with stakes and strings, the beds hold their shape and do not have to be laid out each year. The beds are narrow enough for one to lay out the rows by eye without the time-consuming use of stakes and string every year.

It should be mentioned here that raising the beds increases the growth activity on their surface, a principle which Rudolf Steiner mentioned in his agricultural lectures. After wet periods the increased activity and air circulation result in better control of excess moisture.

### How to Know When to Plant

Planting dates are so variable even in one neighborhood that the only way to be sure of the right time to plant is to watch the neighbors and see when they plant! A friend tells us that in some parts of the world people watch for the ants in spring and plant after they appear, observing that the ants, who live in the ground, know best when the soil is the right condition to work. One soon finds out in a town who are the early planters and who are the ones who wait till too late and then make excuses all summer. By Saint Patrick's Day some may have planted potatoes, and from then until midsummer there is a steady flow of garden activity.

Anyone who has gardened in one place for a few years will develop something like a sixth sense which tells him when the soil is ready to be worked. If you watch the soil conditions closely, — and by "watch" we mean go out and actually feel the soil with your footsteps and with your hands; pick it up, work it in your fingers, smell it, and really notice with all your powers of observation how it is changing from day to day — you will not try to work the soil when it is too wet in the early spring. Soils differ greatly, even in one field. Sandy soil can stand working much earlier than a clay soil which "balls up" and dries out in solid lumps if it is worked when it is too wet. To the experienced hand, soil texture itself will tell when it is time to sow, and absolutely the only way the hand can gain experience is by actual feeling of the soil. We labor this point, because ours is an age which substitutes book learning or verbal discussion for actual experience, and this leads to many errors. A good Bio-Dynamic compost added to the soil will facilitate working the soil early in the spring, partly because it makes the soil blacker and

21

**Annuals: inner arcs**

**Perennials: outside the dotted line**

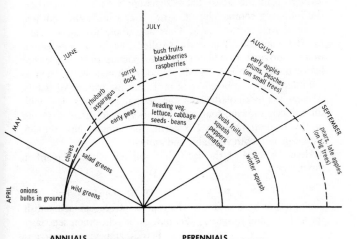

| | ANNUALS _____ | PERENNIALS _ _ _ _ _ _ |
|---|---|---|
| **APRIL** | wild greens, fiddleheads, dandelions | onions: bulbs in ground — few tops appear — chives |
| **MAY** | leaves come out first — salad greens | asparagus, rhubarb |
| **JUNE** | leaves — lettuce, spinach **Lamb's Quarter**<br>seed — early peas<br>roots — early radish, turnip | sorrel, dock |
| **JULY** | leaves — heading lettuce, early cabbage | bush fruits — berries growing on taller canes |
| **AUGUST** | seed — green beans — need warm soil<br>fruits — squash, peppers, tomatoes<br>flowers — broccoli, cauliflower | early apples, plums and peaches on small fruit trees<br>(do not keep well) |
| **SEPT.** | roots — beets<br>seed — corn — grows on tall plant<br>fruit — winter squash — grows on tall vine | late apples and pears on tall trees<br>(good winter keepers) |

**Figure 2.**

richer so it warms up earlier, and partly because the organic matter in the compost helps to distribute and control the moisture in the soil.

Phenomenology

Nature has a definite planting calendar — not printed on

22

paper, but growing, alive in the living landscape, and we human beings can learn to interpret nature's calendar if we will learn to read the signs. These signs apply to any area where the following common plants grow; they will fit the southern states as well as the north. They also apply to England and to other countries. The study is called Phenomenology (sometimes shortened to Phenology): the science of the relations between climatic and periodic biological phenomena, such as the migrations and breeding of birds and the fruiting of plants. A great many scholarly books in several languages deal with the subject, showing that man has always had intense interest in the relation between the earth, the climate and the life on our planet, both vegetable and animal.

Here are some of the facts that will tell when to plant in the spring:

| PHENOMENON IN NATURE | WHAT TO PLANT AT THIS TIME |
|---|---|
| Color begins to show in spring bulbs and forsythia | *Sow:* peas, lettuce, spinach, radish |
| | *Set out:* garlic sets, onion sets, raspberries, grapevines, asparagus, rhubarb, perennial flowering plants. Strawberry plants will make a good start in early spring, whereas they are easily killed in hot dry weather if transplanting is delayed too long. |
| Plum and Peach in bloom (Temperature will average about 45°F. in the shade.) | *Sow:* endive, head lettuce, second sowing of peas |
| | *Set out:* second onion sets |

The outdoor temperature by this time should average about 45°F. in the shade at the time of planting, depending on one's location and wind currents. Thus, if the gardener lives in the valley or half-way up a mountain, it might not be possible for him to establish an exact planting date by the calendar. But the peach and the plum tree will tell him because they

23

will not bloom until the spring's increasing warmth has awakened their blossoms. As the spring advances and other later fruits come into bloom it is safe to sow the more tender plants:

| IN BLOOM | TIME TO SOW |
| --- | --- |
| Apple, Quince, Cherry | All seeds of less hardy plants may |
| Strawberry | be sown after these fruits have |
| Grapevine | bloomed. |

These fruits, especially the grapevine, delay their blooming until there is no longer any danger of killing frosts. Anyone who observes the successive signs of spring and records them every year, will add to this list his own observations to make up his own system for knowing when to sow different kinds of seeds.

Neighbors will recite local proverbs: "Plant corn when the oak leaves are the size of a mouse's ear." In the Midwest they say, "Plant corn when the Red Bud is in bloom." This means not only to plant some corn when the Red Bud comes into bloom, but to continue second and third plantings of corn as long as the Red Bud is blooming. In some places folk say the Brown Thrasher tells when and how to plant corn: "Dig it deep, dig it deep .... Drop it, Drop it ... Cover it up, Cover it up." Since the Brown Thrasher does not return from the South until the sun has warmed the atmosphere in the late spring, he is reputed to be a dependable instructor. A steady, consistent study of the migration and nesting of birds will tell much about the progress of the Spring and of the development of soil conditions in the garden which depend upon temperature.

There are other customs which some people follow to the letter: "Sow potatoes on Saint Patrick's Day." "Sow peas on Good Friday" — which works well if Easter comes early, but not so well if Easter is late and the soil is too warm for peas. An old proverb says "Saint Benedict makes onions thick," referring to the fact that if onions are planted on St. Benedict's Day (March 21st) they will grow robust because of the early moisture and coolness.

24

Until the beginner has gained some experience, he would do well to ask advice of his neighbors or his local hardware store to find out what crops will grow best in his locality. Most vegetables are adapted to grow almost anywhere if they have sufficient moisture and soil nutrients, but some require a long season while others have special requirements which make them unfit for every locality. There is always someone who has a "green thumb" reputation and who will be glad to talk gardening with anyone interested. Don't let too many advisors throw you into a state of confusion; there are as many theories as there are gardeners! Our advice is to choose one system, learn it thoroughly and stick to it carefully for several years before you are tempted to change with the next wind that bows. We can almost guarantee that if you really learn and follow Bio-Dynamics thoroughly, you will find it so complete and so all-embracing that you will not want to change your system. It should be mentioned here that the gardener must first of all follow sound agricultural principles. He must be a good gardener first, and then Bio-Dynamics will help him. He cannot expect Bio-Dynamic preparations and practices to rescue his garden if he neglects it or does not do the best he can every season.

# Seeds

The more seed catalogs one has, the more one can learn by comparing and studying them for all kinds of gardening information. All garden magazines carry advertisements with coupons, and it is easy to send for any number of free seed catalogs. Some of the larger seed houses send not only the usual spring catalog but also a nursery catalog (trees and shrubs) in the winter and a spring bulb catalog in late summer when spring bulbs should be purchased and set out for the following year.

## What Is Meant by Varieties of Seed

It may be well to explain here what the horticulturists mean when they use the words species or kind, and variety: Species or kind refers to a group of plants which possess one or more distinctive characteristics in common, such as cabbage. The cabbage species is then divided into varieties, each of which is a subdivision having a slight variation from the species type. Savoy Cabbage, for instance, has crinkled leaves, Danish Ball Head has a round form, and Flat Dutch is flattened in shape. These are all varieties of the cabbage species.

The catalogs often mention disease-resistant varieties, and these are often good ones for amateurs to start with. Tomatoes of wilt-resistant strains are usually safer to buy. The fact that one variety is noted as wilt-resistant may mean that the variety not so noted is suscepitble to wilt (a disease of tomato plants). The more one studies seed catalogs, the more one notices such factual statements, and the more one can apply that knowledge to make the garden fulfill one's highest hopes.

"Early" and "late" varieties have been developed in many kinds of vegetables, and in this case "early" means maturing in fewer days than the "late" variety. In northern parts of the United States, or in the mountains, the "early" varieties may be the only ones that will mature because of the short growing season. Sometimes the "early" varieties mature two or three weeks sooner than the "late" ones, and this may make the difference between a matured crop and one that is only half-grown when the fall frosts come. Some vegetables, such as tomatoes which require a long growing season between the sowing of the seed and maturing of the fruit, may have to be started indoors or in a cold frame. By buying seed from a seed house reasonably nearby, one is likely to get varieties adapted to that locality. Another point to bear in mind is that seed from the north will grow further south, whereas seed produced in the south will be tender and may not resist a colder northern climate. The same holds true for plants, berries, shrubs and trees. Order from companies to the north of you, but not to the south.

### Hardiness

While you are studying the seed catalogs, you will find mention of the word "hardy" in describing a variety. "Hardy" crops can stand from medium to heavy frosts and they are sometimes sown in the fall and wintered over. In some climates they will be safe from freezing if they are covered with layers of straw or a light mulch (not leaves, because they pack and do not allow any moisture to filter through).

Some "hardy" crops may be sown in the garden very early, although the time should be watched so that the late frost will not nip the seedlings. They include Brussels sprouts, celery, endive, leek, lettuce, corn salad, onions, scallions (need protective covering of straw during the winter), kale, parsnips, mustard and garden cress, salsify, spinach (needs straw protection).

The following seeds will stand from medium to heavy frosts and are called "half-hardy:" beets, broccoli, cabbage, Swiss chard, carrots, cauliflower, curled endive, kohlrabi, head lettuce, peas, radish, turnip, rutabaga.

Others, which will stand no frost at all are called "tender." They include green beans, lima beans, corn, cucumber, egg plant, peppers, pumpkins, okra, marrow, melons, all kinds of squash, tomatoes. (Pumpkins and squash vines are killed by the fall frost, but the fruit is not damaged.)

### Varieties for the Deep Freeze

Most seed catalogs have a symbol which indicates which varieties are best for home freezing. Some vegetables, for instance the tomato, require special treatment and usually are not recommended for freezing. Most vegetables, however, are excellent when frozen and will thus extend the garden food supply throughout the year. Green peas, lima beans, sweet corn, cauliflower, broccoli, asparagus, shredded cabbage, diced beets, sliced leeks, diced parsnips, and chopped parsley and chives are excellent after freezing. Research has shown that vitamins and other food elements are better preserved by freezing than by any other method of preservation. When the family tires of the bumper crop of green beans, it is not difficult to slip some into the freezer to be enjoyed in the winter.

It is of the utmost importance to use "freezing varieties" of seeds if you intend to freeze the produce. One year by mistake we froze some Alaska peas which are not recommended for freezing, and we found out why. They thawed out all right, but they remained solid green spheres with texture like sawdust and no flavor at all, and they were encased in a tough green skin. When some varieties of green beans are frozen, they come out limp and leathery. It is therefore important to plant the freezing varieties, even though one may not always plan to freeze the produce. Then if there should be a surplus, it would be safe to put it into the freezer.

### Vegetables the Family Likes to Eat

When you sit down with the seed catalog to plan the garden for next spring, it is a good idea to have a list of the family's favorite vegetables. Seed catalogs are written to sell seeds, and the mouth-watering descriptions may overpower discretion unless the family's tastes are the first consideration. Too many green beans or a surplus of summer squash may tax any cook's patience and ingenuity.

# How Much of Each Vegetable to Plant

Many seed catalogs include a table which lists the amount of produce to expect from a hundred foot row. Some catalogs even give the approximate production in pounds and relate it to a family of four. These general principles are pretty much the same no matter whether one is a Bio-Dynamic gardener or a follower of the so-called orthodox school of backyard gardening. The 4-H Club leader or your County Agent will be glad to supply you with this kind of information. In general, sixteen feet of leaf lettuce, for instance, is considered sufficient for four people for spring planting. Fall plantings of lettuce should be about twelve feet, planted in August and again in September. Here are some recommended quantities for a family of four:

| VEGETABLE | LENGTH OF ROW |
|---|---|
| Spring leaf lettuce | 16 feet |
| Fall plantings " | 12 feet in August |
| | 12 feet in September |
| Potatoes | 800 feet |
| Onion Sets | 60 feet |
| Radish | 16 feet |
| Cabbage | 100 plants |
| Broccoli | 24 plants |
| Cauliflower | 24 plants |
| Brussels Sprouts | 24 plants |
| Asparagus Roots (Perennial) | 40 roots, set out in April the first year |
| Rhubarb roots " | 12 roots, set out in April the first year |
| Green beans | 20 feet, sow every two or three weeks |
| Sweet corn, early | 40 feet sown around April 15th |
| Sweet corn, early | 100 feet, sown around May 1st |
| Sweet corn, midseason | 100 feet sown May 15th |
| Sweet corn, midseason | 80 feet, sown June 1 |
| Sweet corn, midseason | 80 feet, sown June 15 |
| Sweet corn, late | 80 feet, sown July 15 |
| Muskmelon, cantaloupe | 12 hills, sown when weather is warm |
| Cabbage for fall storage | 24 plants; plant early varieties on June 15th |
| Tomatoes | 12 plants; set out after last frost |

This list is only a suggestion to give a general idea which each family can adapt to its own needs and preferences. The same caution applies here again: plant less rather than more of everything! You will be surprised at the lavish way nature provides, and the tiny pinch of seed that you can hold in your hand will grow and expand beyond your wildest expectations if gardening conditions are right. It is much better to plant small quantities and harvest the produce at its best, than to have a surplus which grows beyond its prime and is useless for food.

One way to insure always having vegetables at their prime is to arrange the sowings successively, so that the crops will ripen in succession. In general all the seed of a certain variety will ripen at the same time, that is, in the same number of days (with some variations: seed sown after midsummer takes longer to mature because of the shortening days). Don't plant a big field of table corn all at once and expect it to be good to eat for a long time (unless you plan on a houseful of summer visitors or a crew to help you can or freeze it.)

It is possible to "stagger" the plantings, putting in some seed as early as possible with other plantings ten days apart to stretch the sweet corn season. This will also give you an opportunity to observe the effects of the season on a single crop. You will notice the results of rain and drought, shorter days, lengthening to the longest days and then the shortening days after the summer solstice. You can also observe, and perhaps record, the unequal growth of the crop, depending on the moon cycles. Full moon and the dark of the moon will be a time of spurting growth which can be measured objectively. A rain storm will also make a noticeable difference in the crop, as will also a considerable temperature change. The backyard gardener learns to notice these details. If he is a student of Bio-Dynamics he will also learn to see the earth's unchangeable patterns and the order in all natural phenomena. Once he learns about soil, moisture, weather and the sun's effect on vegetation, he would do better to throw away the books and learn to study the earth firsthand. Then he will be able to grow luxuriant gardens from his own close contact and understanding of the natural forces at work in our earth and in the cosmos.

### A Large Crop from a Small Patch

A few years ago an enthusiastic gardener, Mr. A. B. Ross, wrote a book titled BIG CROPS FROM LITTLE GARDENS. His main idea is to plant "prior crops" early, a main crop of peas and corn, and "follow crops" last, which will carry the productive season until the hard freezes in the late fall. Even earlier than his "prior crops" are the plants which can be wintered over with protection of straw in the northern climates. Each gardener will have to find out what can be wintered over in his own locality. There will be variations in weather conditions and temperatures caused by mountains, prevailing winds and atmospheric differences of various kinds.

The largest possible crop may be grown on the smallest area by planting alternating rows of peas and corn, eighteen inches apart. The peas are sown in early spring, long before the corn goes into the ground. While the corn rows are still unplanted, they may be used for early, short season vegetables such as onion sets, radishes, lettuce, spinach, mustard, cress and turnips. As these mature, they are used, leaving the corn rows empty and easy to cultivate when it is time to sow corn. On the other hand, the peas are sown very early in spring. After they bear their fruit in June, the dying vines are pulled out. Other seeds are sown in the emptied pea rows and are called "follow crops."

These follow crops benefit from the nitrogen brought into the soil by the roots of the peas. Follow crops like cabbage, cauliflower, lettuce, Brussels sprouts, turnips, Chinese cabbage, which do well in the cool rains of September are difficult to start in the hot summer unless they are shaded and sheltered by some other plants. We have found that it works well to start all these follow crops in the former pea rows by mid-July. After the corn matures and the stalks are pulled out, there is a full-grown fall garden of cabbages and other follow crops, ready to extend the garden season well into the cold weather in the fall. Mr. Ross's book describes this system in detail and we recommend its use as a planting pattern in connection with Bio-Dynamics as a system for composting and general garden care. Mr. Ross has answered all possible objections to his system: for instance, instead of depleting the soil by so many plants, his system continually restores fertility by the presence of peas, legumes, which provide new nitrogen in the soil. We have used this plan for many years, and it works. It should be added that one sometimes needs a diagram of the plantings to locate certain plants in the jungle that is likely to result. This planting plan also adapts itself well to the use of Bio-Dynamic raised beds in the vegetable garden.

# Tools

Every gardener has a right to his own choice of tools. It is well worth the time for careful study to make sure the choices of tools are right for each phase of the work. There are many kinds of tools, some more practical than others. As the gardener becomes more experienced, he learns exactly what works best for him, but some suggestions here may be of help to the beginner.

It is well to get information and prices from several sources to compare both styles of tools and prices. One sometimes has to search nowadays to find simple hand tools for gardening instead of complicated gadgets run by motors. It is sometimes possible to buy good old tools at auctions or second hand sales. These old tools have several advantages: the old steel is often of excellent quality and will sharpen well and hold an edge. The old handles, unless they are so worn that they will easily break, may be straighter and stronger and lighter to lift and carry around the garden.

Power tools have little part in the very small intensive garden, but if one has other areas to cultivate and can afford the outlay for a garden tractor, it is a great help in the initial preparation of the garden area in each year's breaking of the soil. Before making a large investment in power tools it would be well for one to be sure one is going to be an ardent enough gardener to warrant the expense. A word of caution belongs here: Before you purchase a power tool, try several different models and be sure you really want to use such a noisy, weighty mechanical tool in your garden.

The hand tools are even more important than the heavy machinery, for hand cultivation is the way to produce a high degree of soil fertility. Many people like some kind of wheel hoe, cultivator or hand garden plow, either with a large wheel or a double wheel. These come with a variety of attachments, which can be studied from a catalog or tried out in a shop that sells them.

The long handled shovel gives better leverage, but is heavier; the shorter, light "D" handle shovel will work well for most jobs.

A spade is less necessary than a four-pronged spading fork which does good service in digging out sod, and can also lift out plants with less injury to the root than a spade or shovel.

The bow-head rake with 12 or 14 teeth is a more handy size than a wider rake.

The very necessary and useful garden hoe has a number of variations: There is a "Garden Rapid Hoe" with a patented swivel joint which combines weeding and cultivating efficiently in such a way that it is not necessary to walk on the soil that has already been hoed. The scuffle hoe will get into small corners where an ordinary hoe cannot function, especially against a wall or fence.

These are the most essential hoes. A number of others, such as the two-pronged weeding hoe, the Warren or heart-shaped hoe, the narrow nursery hoe, are good and may be personally preferred, but it is better to start with a few and learn all their possible adaptations. It is also possible to start with a big hoe and have a machinist reduce it in size, then sharpen it again, to lighten it.

Another tool, a sort of cross between a hoe and a rake, is called by various names, including "crile," "speedy cultivator," or "potato hook." This is the quickest tool for breaking the soil surface after a rain. With it the whole garden can be gone over in a short time, an important fact, since the crumbly surface so valuable in maintaining soil moisture can be attained only if the job is done at just the right moment with the right degree of dryness. Having the tines bent at right angles gives a good grip for pulling the tool through the clods to break them. The motion of pulling is slightly less hard on the back muscles than lifting which is necessary with a spade or spading fork. Since the tines are narrower than a rake, it takes less strength to pull it through the soil. The narrow width of the tool makes it satisfacory also for shaking sods which sometimes need to be attacked vigorously. A spading fork is better for shaking out heavy clay sods.

One rule to remember: "Lift the tool before you buy it" and "Feel the 'heft' of it". Turn it around, pretend you are using it right there in the store, to make sure you do not buy a tool that will always feel clumsy in your hands. A tool that feels awkward while you are buying it, will remain unused when you go to work in the garden. It might be observed here that it is a great temptation to run off to town to buy a better tool, but often a new tool is actually no better than the old one. What one really needs is greater perserverance with the old tool!

For close-range weeding and cultivating down at the level of the plants, there are several short handled tools: a trowel of one piece steel blade and shank is worth the extra cost, whereas a cheap, thin one will soon break. A transplanting trowel has a narrow blade. Many gardeners use improvised tools for transplanting. A broad-bladed kitchen knife of old steel works well and shines with use. A "finger weeder" or "five finger" helps scratch the soil close to the plant stems. The sharp kitchen knife will cut off the weed seedlings when they are tender and will scuff up a dust mulch at the same time. A sharp and sturdy knife is indispensible for many jobs the gardener has to do: to sharpen stakes and cut strings and clip off stray branches and twigs. A pair of small pruning clippers carried in a pocket at all times is incentive to snip and clip and prune small branches, which helps keep plants and shrubs in good condition.

A tool called a "Cape Cod Weeder" which was originally used to weed cranberry bogs is the best tool we know for weeding and cultivating at close range. It consists of a 5/8" strap of steel, seven or eight inches long, set in a handle. About one and a half inches from the end it is bent at a right angle. This tool acts like a steel "index finger" bent at a right angle which hooks around even the strongest weeds and cuts them off. The same tool is available with a long handle and is excellent for weeding without bending.

In the small garden a sprinkling can may take the place of a garden hose, but is necessary anyway. Buy one of medium size — two or three gallons is ample and will not be so heavy to carry when full. New models of cans come out every year, some of them made of plastic, which is lightweight and easy to carry. One model of watering can for small jobs has a hole in the handle which makes it very easy to fill from a faucet. These are all small details to study and weigh before making purchases. Incidentally, in some garden literature one reads about watering with "the rose." This is the horticulural name for the nozzle fitted into the end of the watering can, which divides the stream as it sprinkles.

Spraying on a small scale is best done with a bucket pump or a trombone type spray, also used with a bucket. These are not difficult to clean, are of lighter weight and easier to handle than the compressed air tank sprayers. A bucket also is necessary. Small pint or quart hand sprayers are not sufficient for a garden. When using Bio-Dynamic sprays it is most important to keep sprayers scrupulously clean and in tip-top condition. One would even do well to have several small sprayers to use with different Bio-Dynamic teas and sprays. (For more detailed information on this entire subject see the pamphlet on BIODYNAMIC SPRAYS by Evelyn Speiden Gregg.)

Several baskets will be needed, from the ordinary bushel basket for collecting weeds, to the basket with handle for gathering the harvest or for carrying seedlings while transplanting. A small cart can be loaded with all the tools one plans to use for the day. It is also easy to pull the cart into a protecting shed or garage when there is a sudden shower.

Even with a good cart, a wheelbarrow is a necessity. Here again, weight is an important factor and probably the wooden barrow with removable sides is the most generally useful.

When the array of new tools is finally assembled, it may be well to use a bright colored paint to put an identifying band on each one. It also helps to have a definite place to store each tool. If this is on a wall, one can paint the shape of the tool where it is to hang. Thus a missing item is quickly noticed. A pegboard with hooks makes an excellent place to keep garden tools. To put away a used tool before it has been scraped clean and shining is said to indicate a poor gardener. In any case a clean, oiled, sharpened tool makes for much greater gardening efficiency. Especially in the fall when outdoor work is largely over, it is well to go over all tools to clean them thoroughly, oil the metal parts, and if necessary, paint the wood.

Whatever tools you plan to use, if they can be kept near the garden there will be more incentive to keep the gardening work well done from day to day. In the heat of the summer the cultivating itself may be so arduous that an additional outlay of energy to carry tools from the cellar to the garden may make one put off garden work completely. It is better to keep tools on the ground level. Keeping wrenches, pliers, oil cans and a whetstone and file as well as sandpaper, wax and paint where the tools are stored will save steps on busy days.

## Soil Analysis and Lime

The only way to know exactly what your soil requires, is to have a soil analysis made. Full details on this can be obtained from the Biochemical Research Laboratory, Spring Valley, New York. Your county agent, who is connected with the Extension Department of your State University, will also make soil tests, but since these tests are mostly concerned with a quantitative analysis of the elements present in your soil they will not give as much practical information as a test from a biochemical laboratory, which tests for immediate availability and for the living qualities in the soil.

Some agricultural advisors take it for granted that every soil needs lime, but this is not always the case, and the use of lime can be seriously overdone. If lime is used it should always be with compost, not instead of it. Be sure you have a soil analysis before you add lime to your soil. It has been the experience of many amateur gardeners in many localities that when they use good Bio-Dynamic compost they can raise excellent crops in soil which theoretically may be too acid. The compost seems to act as a buffer to even out excesses or deficiencies in lime in all soils.

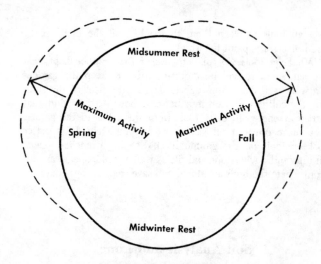

## IT IS IMPORTANT FOR GARDENERS TO KNOW
## THAT SOIL BACTERIA GO THROUGH YEARLY CYCLES

This explains why **soil samples** should be
taken in April or October and why it is almost
impossible to do any gardening at Midsummer
and Christmas.

Figure 3.

### Soil Textures

The texture and quality of a soil is such a technical subject that we can only touch upon it briefly, but we can speak as amateurs who have used the Bio-Dynamic Method intensively in four different types of soil over a period of twenty years.

We have learned by experience that a garden plot worked entirely by hand tools does not become hard and impacted. Each year the soil seems better aerated and feels softer and spongier as we walk on it. After two years' application of Bio-Dynamic compost, we have never had to do any spring plowing. (This does not apply to sod ground or to ground heavily covered with weeds where a new garden is to be made.) We use an old bayonet point, now made into a garden tool. We draw a string tight to indicate the location of the row, and then scratch a furrow with the bayonet point and drop in the seeds. This is possible because the Bio-Dynamic compost has enlivened the soil, which becomes light and well aereated. This has been our experience in all four locations, once in sandy soil (which incidentally acts as a non-conductor of frost) twice in loëss soil in the midwest, and again in a loamy soil on top of a mountain. This experience makes us say, from the amateur's standpoint, that Bio-Dynamic compost will benefit any kind of soil and will greatly simplify the working of the soil for the gardener.

We have also learned to make use of the winter's colds and frosts to condition harder sections of soil in the garden. Where the soil is rough or more recently cultivated, we spade it up and leave it over the winter in rough clods. In early spring, as soon as the snow has melted and the surface water has evaporated, if you look closely at a clod left upended over the winter, you will actually see the effect of the cold. The clod will still be standing, a lump higher than the surrounding soil. But it will show signs of wear where it has been weathered by wind and rain and snow and frost. Around the clod, especially on the windward side, you will see a fine sprinkling of soil which has been loosened by frost and has been blown off by the wind. You will recognize it by the pulverized particles lying in the troughs between the clods. This is silent but strong evidence that cold and wind are two powerful forces at work in the world of nature, even though we do not always pay attention to them.


## Dressing the Soil: Bio-Dynamic Compost

It is to be noted here that we shall not deal extensively with the technical aspects of Bio-Dynamic compost or the BD Compost Starter. These are both highly scientific subjects which the amateur is not equipped to handle. But, as enthusiastic gardeners, we know from long experience what happens when these materials are actually put to use in our own gardens.

The following pages therefore give information which is based on our experience.

Making and using Bio-Dynamic compost, like many other arts, might well be the subject of a highly technical volume, but here we have tried to write only from our own experiences in following Bio-Dynamic practices.

The use of compost for fertilizer has several advantages which gear directly into the family life of busy Americans of the twentieth century. First, the addition of compost improves the tilth, that is, the condition of the soil so that it is possible to work the garden in early spring with hand tools. Thus it is possible to get the garden planted earlier without having to wait for someone to come and plow. Early planting is essential for the gardener who wants to get the most out of his garden before the summer heat begins. Early planting also enables families to get an early crop of summer vegetables before they leave for summer vacations.

When compost is used, there is less need for watering in a dry season. The old proverb says "Nitrogen is water in time of drought," and nitrogen is present in the compost, especially if some barnyard manure has been incorporated in the compost heaps.

The incorporation of compost in the garden makes the soil darker in color, which in turn allows it to absorb the heat of the sun's rays so that the garden soil warms up earlier in the spring. This enables the family to take advantage of the early spring moisture which evaporates as the heat grows more intense with the progressing season. It also enables the family to gather vegetables earlier, thus helping the food budget. By planting early and planning successive crops to take care of the late vegetables, it is possible even as far north as Massachusetts to harvest garden produce for about seven months of the year.

Finally, compost-fed gardens seem to produce healthier plants, and there is no question about the better flavor and keeping qualities of produce grown with Bio-Dynamic compost.

Compost-fed soil attracts earthworms which in their search for food turn and churn the topsoil, bringing to the surface the minerals which lie deep in the soil, thus making the minerals available to the feeder roots of the plants.

Our ideal should always be to leave the soil better than we find it, and from many laboratory tests we know that Bio-Dynamic compost is more beneficial to the soil than any other kind of treatment. The fact that it utilizes many kinds of waste materials and turns them into a useful, nourishing fertilizer is a strong point in its favor. It is also a convenience, when one has finished pulling a big pile of weeds from a flower bed, to have one definite place to leave those weeds, where they will gradually turn into usable compost for next year's garden. The same is true of the contents of the garbage pail, if there is no garbage collection in the community. If the compost is properly layered with earth and an occasional light sprinkling of lime, and a bacterial starter added to speed the chemical changes, there will be no offensive odors to make the neighbors complain. Adding hen manure or barnyard manure, or both, to the other materials that go into the compost will help to speed fermentation.

We know, as a result of many tests, that Bio-Dynamic compost is beneficial to all kinds of soils. If the garden is sandy and the moisture runs down through the sand as fast as it falls from the sky, the addition of compost will make the soil absorbent like a sponge, so it will hold the water. If the soil is composed largely of clay which bakes into hard clods when the sun shines, or worse yet, opens into deep cracks because the sun draws the moisture out, adding compost will make the soil absorb and hold the water. The added organic material in minute particles will separate the clay particles and make the clods crumbly. The crumbly surface is easy to hoe, making a dust mulch, through which the sun cannot draw the moisture. Thus cracks are eliminated. These observations are the result of our actual experience in using Bio-Dynamic compost in these two differing types of soil.

One section of soil had been neglected and the weeds grew waist high. By using Bio-Dynamic compost, the section was brought into a state of higher fertility — so much so that a neighboring farmer said one day, "Your piece of soil is different...It grows things better than any other place on this farm." There was no secret about it, except that we had used carefully made Bio-Dynamic compost, and during the three seasons we worked it, that ground had no other treatment than Bio-Dynamic compost and cultivation.

## Location of the Compost Heap

The first consideration in making compost is where to locate the compost heap. If possible it should be on the north side of a building or a thick row of trees, preferably hardwoods, but beyond reach of the tree roots. The sunshine should be filtered so that the hot sun will not draw out the moisture. It is possible to grow a protective shade of sunflowers or pole beans or even to let tall weeds grow up to shade the heap. Weed roots should not grow into the heap, because they steal the good food elements and draw out the moisture. Squash and watermelon vines grow well in the soil at the base of the heap and the vines may be trained over the top so that the vine leaves provide shade for the heap, but no plants should actually grow on top.

Through the years people sensitive to natural facts have observed that birch, elderberry, alder and hazelnut shrubs are especially good to grow near the compost yard for the shade they give and for the beneficial effect they have on the soil. There is something in the roots of these particular trees which contributes to the quality of the finished compost. The roots aid in breaking down the materials in the compost. Simply sink a spade into the soil around an elderberry bush in the woods and watch the spade almost disappear in the soft, fluffy topsoil which the elderberry has created around its roots in the area known as the rhizosphere.

### The Time to Build a Compost Heap

The time to begin to build a compost heap is right now!

At least now is the time to start collecting piles of compostable materials, wherever they are encountered. We always have piles of weeds and clippings tucked away out of sight, with baskets of leaves and soil from discarded house plants, old flowers, Christmas greens and any other organic materials that once were living, growing plants. Although the actual compost heaps are not constructed until spring or fall, the materials that go into them are accumulating constantly.

An ideal time to build a compost heap is in the fall when the garden is cleaned up and made ready for the winter. If bacterial compost starter is put into the heap and it is left to absorb the winter rains and snows, the finished compost will be ready to use about the middle of the following summer.

In early spring when the tops of perennials are clipped off and the yard is cleaned up for the summer, there are piles of clippings and materials suitable for composting. Therefore spring is also a time to build compost, and by late fall a heap built in April will be ready to spread on the garden for a compost mulch. The bacterial action in the soil and in the compost heaps is at its height in spring and fall. It is at its lowest ebb in the hot summer and the cold winter, and you will find that in the two latter seasons you will have no interest whatsoever in getting out and building compost heaps. This should not be a cause for concern because when the season comes around again, you will be ready to collect materials and build compost heaps once more.

## What Should Go into a Compost Heap?

We are always astonished at the available quantities of compostable materials. Every time we start to collect for a new heap, we think there is very little to put into it, but by the time it is collected, there is always plenty. Literally, almost everything under the sun can be used: coffee grounds, egg shells (which contain lime and sulphur), corn cobs, cabbage stalks, celery tops, tea leaves, peanut shells and all kinds of table scraps, including grapefruit and orange peels. We always empty the vacuum cleaner bag onto the compost because the contents are made up of dust which is only misplaced topsoil, hair, and the fuzz off the rugs, either wool or cotton. Nutshells and tropical fruit peels may bring some of the minerals and trace elements from another part of the earth. Lobsters which died in transit from the State of Maine added minerals from the Atlantic Ocean to a midwest biodynamic compost heap! Once an old cocoa fiber rug ended its long and useful career in a compost heap.

## Windbreaks

Protection from the wind is so important that it cannot be emphasized too often. It may be possible to locate the compost heap where trees and shrubs or a building will break the prevailing wind. It may be possible to plant a few shrubs at each end of an enclosure to make a protected compost yard where fertilizing materials can be made for many years to come. If compost is kept in a secluded spot there is no need of any complaints from the neighbors. It should be stated that well-made compost does not have an offensive smell. The kitchen garbage which goes into it has a bad odor only while it is being dumped, if it is immediately covered with earth and perhaps dusted very lightly with a slight trace of lime. Even barnyard manure loses its odor after a short time in the fresh air and sunshine and contact with the earth. Anyone who had made compost will testify that the finished product smells sweet and earthy like the woods after a spring rain.

## Compost Yard Should Be Near the Kitchen

If the compost heap is built as close as possible to the kitchen door, it is not difficult to see to it that every day's garbage is carried out and added to the pile. If a small quantity of bacterial starter is added to the garbage in the kitchen, the heap is automatically "innoculated" with the "yeast" which speeds up fermentation and makes the heap break down faster. We have found that by spreading an inch or two of good top-soil in the bottom of the garbage pail, the odor is kept down as much as it is with soap and water. It is not completely eliminated either way, but the earth seems to absorb most of it, and when everything is returned to the

43

compost pile, none of the good bacterial starter has been lost or destroyed with soap or detergents.

## Plan for Transportation of Compost Before You Build

Before you build your compost heap, be sure that it is in such a place that it can easily be moved to the garden with a wheelbarrow or trailer, if it has to be moved at all. A little planning beforehand will save many hours of hard labor carrying the compost in bushel baskets because the gate is too narrow to accommodate the wheelbarrow. Garden paths should be made wide enough to accommodate various carts and wheelbarrows, which speed up the work. This is something to remember when planning the rows for seeding in the spring: the mature plant will cover a large circle, of which the location of the tiny seed is only the center!

## Water

Since water is an absolute essential, it is necessary to build the compost heap in a place that can be reached by a hose. Rainwater is better than city water and it may be simple to put a wooden barrel under a downspout from the house. The same quality of softness which makes rainwater best for shampooing the hair, makes it best for watering house plants or for watering the compost heap. It is unfortunate that we now have a problem with radio-active fallout in our rain water.

If the compost is allowed to dry out, much of the bacterial action is stopped and some of the bacteria may die. Some however, will become dormant and when the heap is watered again, the bacterial action will recommence. The heap should be thoroughly soaked when it is built. Later it should be kept at the moisture of a wrung-out sponge, not wet enough to squeeze water out, but not really dry. After one has made Bio-Dynamic compost, one gets a feeling for the right amount of moisture to put into it. The experience of a couple of seasons will help you to judge water content. It is well to dig into the end of the heap once in awhile to see if it has enough moisture, because the inside will not be as dry as the outer layers. With a shovel cut a slice off the end of the heap, down through the several layers so that you can see the texture down through the heap. Grasping a handful from near the bottom will enable you to feel the amount of moisture in the compost. When squeezed in the hand, the compost should feel damp and should retain the imprint of your fingers. It should not be dry and crumbly, nor wet and soggy. After cutting through the surface to test the condition of the inside, always replace the outer covering of the surface to protect the interior from sun and wind.

### BD Compost Starter

We have used the BD Compost Starter purchased by mail for our Bio-Dynamic compost heaps. We usually order several ounces at a time and have it on hand for building compost heaps both in spring and in the fall. The starter is dehydrated and does not have to be refrigerated. It comes with complete directions for use.

These are the directions we follow: the evening before we start to build the compost heap, we put three tablespoons of starter in an old cup. We then add rainwater, a little at a time, stirring until the starter is moist but not wet. This is allowed to stand overnight. Next morning the cup of starter is diluted in several gallons of rainwater and this is sprinkled on the compost with every layer. We use a whisk broom to sprinkle the water so that it is thoroughly distributed in fine mist throughout the heap.

### Bio-Dynamic Preparations

Before Dr. Pfeiffer developed the BD Compost Starter we used to use the so-called "Bio-Dynamic preparations" which were indicated by Dr. Steiner. Many of us still use the preparations for small backyard Bio-Dynamic compost heaps. Since this is too technical a subject to be treated here, the reader is advised to get the pamphlet titled BIODYNAMIC SPRAYS by Evelyn Speiden Gregg; this deals with the Bio-Dynamic preparations and also gives further information about the BD Compost Starter.

Usually we have several compost heaps in progress, some of which are built up little by little as we add materials every day or two. We also build one or two heaps which are completed in one day. We always try to get the job done as quickly as possible, but it takes several hours to construct one large heap. All the materials are assembled, and we have the BD Compost Starter prepared the night before. Dressed for the job, we gather wheelbarrow, hoes, shovels, pitchforks and whatever else will be needed, including a hose if the weather is dry.

The word "heap" may give a false impression. To be at its best, compost should not be thrown together in haphazard fashion, but should be laid down carefully in well-planned layers. First decide how large the heap is to be. We have found six feet by ten feet a good dimension. Dig the space to the depth of the shovel, keeping the dug-out soil in a pile at one side where it will be available for a covering later. Build the first layer of some heavy material next to the ground. Hard weed stalks or tough weedy brush lift the pile somewhat from the earth and allow a little drainage of moisture and circulation of air.

The layers are built up, repeating the same sequence over and over, until the pile is about four feet high.

This is the sequence of the layers:

1. Three to six inches of straw, leaves, weeds or other vegetable material.

2. An inch of hen manure, barn dressing (the urine-saturated straw whjch was used for bedding the cattle is also considered as manure.)

3. An inch or two of topsoil, depending on the texture of the soil more if it is sandy, less if it is heavier with clay.

4. A very fine sprinkling of lime.

The moistened BD Compost Starter dissolved in rainwater is sprinkled on each layer in order to distribute it evenly. Although the amount seems insignificant the bacteria are powerful and will multiply by the billions as the compost ripens.

Layers 1, 2, 3, and 4 should be repeated, building each layer slightly smaller than the one below it to make the sides of the heap slope inward toward the top. The layers should be built up to height of four feet high with sides sloping slightly inward and the top flat or slightly hollowed.

The top is slightly hollowed out to form a trough running the length of the heap to catch and hold the rain and the snow. Every two linear feet of a heap of this size will represent approximately one ton of finished compost. If the heap is about four feet high when first finished, it will shrink to about one and one half or two feet when it is ripe. The outside of the heap should be covered with a thin layer of earth which forms a skin and protects the heap from drying out too fast. Experience with the kind of soil in your garden can tell you exactly how thick to make this skin. If it is too thin, the wind will evaporate the moisture through the skin and the compost inside will dry out. If it is too thick, it will be too heavy and in a wet season the compost inside will remain wet and soggy. In a hot, dry, windy climate it may be necessary to cover the heap with straw or hay or even cornstalks to insulate and keep it cool and moist inside. In a dark rainy season it may be necessary to punch holes with a crowbar to let in the air. Only actual experience with the feel of well-made compost will tell what it needs. But observation is a good teacher, and one learns quickly to recognize the conditions and to know what to do. If the compost pile feels springy when you step lightly upon the edge, it is probably in good condition, fermenting inside and carrying on its own life through the action of the living bacteria within.

These directions assume that you have collected piles of materials and that you build the compost heap all in one day. It is also practical to build up one end of the pile and add to it every day as table scraps and lawn clippings come to hand. If some lime and earth are kept nearby, they can be sprinkled on each layer of garbage, the lime first — but very sparingly — and the earth last to make sufficient covering to keep dogs, mice, and flies away. Using BD Compost Starter in a pepper shaker and adding it to the garbage as it leaves the kitchen,

47

renders the materials inoffensive almost immediately and uninteresting to dogs. The latter will not trouble a compost heap once the process of fermentation is under way. If necessary a large piece of poultry netting covering the heap will keep dogs and hens from scratching in it. If it is built up day by day, it is especially important to see that the layers are damp when laid down and that it does not dry out completely before it is finished. It is better not to have to soak it with water after it has dried out.

If bacterial starter is not used, fermentation will still take place, but it will be haphazard and may not completely permeate the heap. In such a case the temperature of the heap may rise rather high at first (124-150F.), but it will cool down later. If such a heap seems to be standing still and not decomposing fast enough, it may be turned with a pitchfork. The exposure of the interior to oxygen speeds up the process of decomposition, but it may also cause too much combustion and burn away much of the goodness in the heap. If the heap gets too hot, it may be cooled down by wetting with a hose.

### Sheet Composting Not Recommended

Some may object to the labor that goes into building the compost heap. As an alternative they advocate digging garbage and refuse directly into the garden soil. This is called sheet composting. It has been used widely, but the gardener who makes an attempt to do the very best with his facilities will do well to avoid this rather unseemly practice. The reason is that the decomposing materials, raw, in the soil will spread odors of decomposition and disease and fungus directly into the soil. The fermentation in a properly built heap will take care of these undesirable elements. But if the offal is placed directly in the soil there can be no fermentation to devour and transform such rubbish without a detrimental effect on the next year's garden crop. It can be demonstrated in the laboratory that the bacteria which have to work to decompose the materials cannot at the same time help the new crop to grow. Thus time is wasted because it takes one year for the bacteria to decompose the added materials, and the plants that year suffer as a result. This is even true of green manuring crops which are plowed back into the soil too soon before the planting of a crop.

## Barrel Method of Making Compost

A magazine article was written for city dwellers who want to make compost but who do not want to risk offending their neighbors, or who have a very small space to devote to compost. It advocates a bottomless barrel with tight fitting lid on top, set in a convenient spot in the garden. Fill it with kitchen waste about six inches (paper, glass, and tin cans, of course, do not go into any compost heap). Put in a layer of soil, preferably rich garden soil which will act as yeast. Add a layer of weeds, grass clippings, leaves, and sprinkle very lightly with lime. By the time the barrel is full, it may be lifted off the material inside and placed in a space nearby where it may be filled again. By moving the barrel along a straight line and alternatively filling it and emptying it, a continuous compost heap will be created with the first-made compost ready to use first. The frequency of moving the barrel depends on the supply of material for filling it. Keeping the barrel in constant use and moving it regularly will insure a constant supply of plant food for garden and house plants. If you add earthworms, or attract them by various means, they will speed up the process of digesting the raw materials. Even if you do not add earthworms, they will eventually come as the soil becomes richer and more attractive to them. This is an excellent way to dipose of garbage and at the same time turn it into something of value for the soil. A tight-fitting lid prevents dogs and rats from getting into the barrel, and the addition of a little lime will help prevent any unpleasant odor. If BD Compost Starter is used with a salt shaker in the kitchen before the garbage is taken out, the fermentation process should be well started. A wooden barrel should be used if possible, to allow the circulation of air which is important to encourage certain beneficial bacteria.

Evidently some industrialist has been impressed with the alarming waste of materials which should be returned to the soil but which are now being sent down the drains by the garbage disposal units. He has invented a garbage eliminator, based on the principles of the barrel method of making compost. It consists of a metal barrel tapering in shape, to be filled and moved to another part of the garden. It has been sold for something less than fifty dollars and should be satisfactory in a neighborhood where the barrel method may not be suitable.

### How Long Before Compost Is Ready for Use?

After the Bio-Dynamic compost heap is built, it begins to settle and to ripen while the bacterial action is taking place inside. In about six months in moderate weather, longer in a cold winter, and a shorter time in summer, when you dig into the pile, you will find fluffy, dark brown soil which looks and smells like the topsoil in the woods under the trees (which is the ideal condition of soil we are attempting to duplicate). Even if there is still some straw or leaf structure visible, it will quickly crumble when dug into the earth. A compost is ready when it has an earthy odor and the original structure of the source material has disappeared. In an incredibly short time you will notice that many earthworms have suddenly appeared, unless you were building on hard-packed soil where there were no earthworms. It is well to get this compost out of the heap and into the gaarden as soon as possible so that its goodness may be distributed into the garden soil. Don't let it wait too long, or it will return to the soil. Your next compost heap should be built on the site of the first one to utilize all the rich earth beneath. If you add some of the old compost in layers when you are building the new pile, this will hasten the fermentation in the new pile. When the material in the compost pile is thoroughly broken down, it becomes humus and it should be incorporated into the topsoil in the garden to promote the growth of vegetables and flowers.

# The Uses of Ripe Compost

Finished compost may be spread on the garden area in the spring and harrowed or plowed in with a shallow plow. We prefer to have the compost sprinkled on the garden beds before they are spaded in the late fall or winter, and left for the frost to work into the soil. This frost action eliminates the need for plowing if the soil is spaded and left rough in the fall. Compost may be carried in a wheelbarrow to the flower borders where a trowelful will give a lift to any single plant that needs encouragement. Adding a compost mulch of half rotted compost to the perennial borders in our very clayey soil, improved the tilth of that clay to an unbelievable extent in three years.

After sowing seed in drills in the vegetable garden, we always cover up the seed with a thick sprinkling of compost, thicker in the case of the heavy feeders. It is amazing how little compost it takes to produce impressive results; for instance, we once had a lawn area which was sparse, thin, and unresponsive. At that time we had very little compost to spare for lawn use, but we did sprinkle about one eighth inch of compost as far as it would go over that grass, which in return showed marked improvement.

Houseplants are most grateful for being watered with rainwater in which a very small amount of compost has been soaked. African violets thrive if planted in straight compost.

Certain vegetables like carrots, lettuce, beets, and radishes which must grow rapidly to be tender, may be helped with a "shot" of compost water. These rather fine, delicately flavored vegetables should be given plenty of finely separated, well decomposed compost. Rose bushes should be fed in the spring with well rotted compost, but in the fall they should be mulched and protected from the cold with coarser material which has not completely broken down. There is a general rule to follow in the use of compost: if a plant is strong and stocky in nature, give it half-broken down compost. If it is delicate and sweet-scented, like the rose or the carrot, give it

51

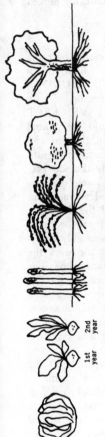

**Examples:**

|   | 1st 2nd year |   |   |   |
|---|---|---|---|---|

## A GENERAL RULE FOR COMPOST REQUIREMENTS

| ANNUALS | BIENNIALS | PERENNIALS | SHRUBS | ORCHARD TREES | FOREST TREES |
|---|---|---|---|---|---|
| LETTUCE tender and succulent — plant develops and matures seed in one season, then dies | BEET tough enough to stand winter — matures seed second year | ASPARAGUS rugged roots which are hard to kill — comes up every year from root | FORSYTHIA delicate form but woody structure | APPLE TREE woody form but small stature | OAK TREE heavy wood structure in timber — stands against weather for years |

## COMPOST-FERTILIZER REQUIREMENTS

| ANNUALS | BIENNIALS | PERENNIALS | SHRUBS | ORCHARD TREES | FOREST TREES |
|---|---|---|---|---|---|
| need plenty of soil food to grow quickly, mature and set seed in one season — manure compost | need a steady supply of good compost each year | need a new supply of good compost — some perennials like peonies and rhubarb like a bushel of manure compost per plant | need a sprinkling of compost every year — not too much | fertilize in a ring under the drip line — put good soil in hole when tree is transplanted with well rotted earthy compost — not manure compost — Dip in 500 to stimulate root growth | minimum amount of fertilizer — no raw manure or raw organic matter |

Figure 4.

52

only old compost that is well seasoned and thoroughly broken down.

### How Much Compost to Use

Bio-Dynamic compose should be scattered evenly over the ground in the garden area before it is plowed, harrowed or spaded, at the rate of ONE PINT OR ONE POUND of compost to every TWO SQUARE FEET of area, or

ONE WHEELBARROW LOAD to an area SEVEN FEET SQUARE. It should be raked or harrowed into the ground immediately, not left on the surface to dry in the sun and the wind. The sooner the food material is incorporated into the soil, the less goodness is lost. Immediately the soil bacteria will start to work the compost into the topsoil to vitalize the seed bed. After one season of using Bio-Dynamic compost on your garden, you will be able to feel the difference in the texture of the soil. The second year it will be easier to handle. The third year you will find it thoroughly enjoyable and not at all difficult to rake, to spade, and work the topsoil, provided of course that it is not worked when it is too wet and sticky. We always notice when we use Bio-Dynamic compost that we can walk in the garden soon after a rainstorm; the compost seems to act like a sponge, absorbing and distributing the excess moisture so it does not lie in puddles on the surface. Also we have no problem of excessive-run-off after a heavy shower.

For newly-developed soil, it would be permissible to use more compost per square foot than was recommended in the foregoing paragraph. Fortunately there is absolutely no danger of burning plants by using too much compost, as there is with all kinds of manures. Compost is a living material and the bacteria in it continue to grow and multiply when they get into the garden soil, thus enlivening and enriching their surroundings by their own efforts.

Once fertility has been established, the garden or lawn can be maintained with smaller amounts of compost. But every garden needs some kind of fertilization every year.

If you do not yet have Bio-Dynamic compost made and are forced to use manure, it should be handled somewhat differently. It should be allowed to ferment and age in a pile, preferably covered from the weather, before it is added to the soil. The reason is that the soil bacteria have to break down the food materials before they can begin to make the plants grow. Putting fresh manure or any other undigested material into the earth, as explained above, may slow down plant growth for the first season while the bacteria are busy breaking down the new material. Fresh manure may be added in the fall and wintered over. The following season the soil will benefit greatly from the broken-down material. Except in special cases, however, it is better to add the manure in layers to the compost pile as you build it.

It can never be emphasized too often, nor too emphatically, that cow manure is absolutely essential for good fertility, and if possible should always be added to every compost heap.

## Preparing the Seed Bed

There is ample information in current newspapers, garden magazines and government bulletins on how to prepare the soil for planting. Briefly, for the first year the soil is first plowed to turn over the topsoil and then harrowed with a series of disks or teeth to cut the sod into small pieces. As we have explained above, after the first year or two, the small garden hardly needs plowing with a heavy plow. Especially if one uses raised Bio-Dynamic beds, it is possible to spade up, or simply to rake one bed at a time, instead of waiting for a plow to come.

In the spring most farmers are so busy that they will keep the small gardener waiting until the first planting days have passed. If the plowing was done in the fall, the garden is ready in early spring for planting. The main thing in spring is not to work the soil while it is too wet. DO NOT EVEN WALK IN THE GARDEN IF ANY MUD STICKS TO YOUR BOOTS. As soon as the soil is dry enough to work, it should be pulverized to a depth of about five inches. It is possible to rake out the rough scraps of vegetation and small stones to make it easier to run the furrow to receive the seeds.

We emphasize that one should not work in the garden when the soil is wet because serious damage can be done and the soil will not recover for the rest of the season. Test it every day with your hands. If the soil holds the impression of your fingers when you squeeze a handful, it is too wet and should not be worked for a day or two. Then one day the handful of soil will fall apart in your hand and will crumble and drop out of your fist without retaining the imprint of your fingers. This is the day to start work.

### Preparing for Planting

Begin by collecting in one place, or in the cart or wheelbarrow, all the tools needed for preparing the soil and putting in the seeds. The tools should include a garden tractor if you use one, and

a rake or crile to loosen clods
a yardstick to measure distances between rows
a hoe for making furrows, or the handle of some other tool will do
stakes to mark rows, with heavy, light-colored string
a hatchet to sharpen the stakes if necessary
a jacknife
seeds in their packets
a seeder, if you need one
labels
pencils
clipboard with your garden plan

Some gardeners like to write into the garden plan what they intend to do on a given day, instead of trying to remember and write it in after it is done. From experience we know that outside in the sun and the wind and the excitement of the springtime, it is very hard to decide just which seeds to plant where. One gets along much faster if the garden plan is well defined and ready to follow.

## Plan of a Biodynamic Garden with Raised Beds

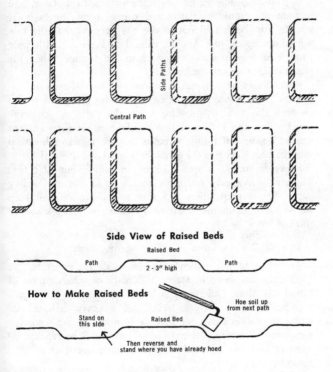

Side Paths

Central Path

### Side View of Raised Beds

Raised Bed

Path    2 - 3" high    Path

### How to Make Raised Beds

Hoe soil up from next path

Stand on this side    Raised Bed

Then reverse and stand where you have already hoed

Figure 5.

# Making Raised Beds

In a small garden it is enough to lay out the plan of the paths, then hoe the soil from paths up onto the beds, standing in a path opposite and hoeing the topsoil towards you over the bed as you go down each path. The higher you can make the raised bed, the greater will be the growth activity.

It is also possible to go down the path with a shovel and pile up soil from the paths and throw it on the beds. If you do this, be careful not to dig too deep so that the subsoil comes up on top. Also be careful to keep the path wide enough for you to stand and walk in the summer when the plants hang over from the beds.

For a larger garden, run a power tool over the entire surface to break it into fine particles. Then lay out paths to run between the beds. By treading down the paths as you work day by day, the beds will rise higher because they are not pressed down. Soil from the paths may be raked or hoed up over the beds whenever the garden is worked or cultivated.

However you go about it, keep in mind your objective, which is to raise each bed a few inches above the surrounding paths. Spring preparation and summer cultivation will keep the soil level upon the raised beds if you always work toward this end.

### Staking Out the Rows and Sowing the Seeds

According to the garden plan you made on paper on the clipboard, now drive in stakes and mark off the location of actual seed rows. Different people use different tools for making the rows. Two strong stakes and a heavy, light-colored string are requirements for making furrows for the seed. Remember: if the furrow is crooked, the row will be crooked all summer and you will feel a little embarrassment every time someone else notices it!

Directions on each seed packet give exact instructions for the depth to sow the seed. After a little experience it will be a simple process to set the stakes, run the length of the string with a hoe or the handle of a tool to make a shallow furrow, run back, shaking the seeds from the envelope into the furrow one at a time (this is the ideal!) run back, drawing loose soil or a layer of Bio-Dynamic compost over the seeds in the furrow. Finally, tread the row — barefoot — to firm the soil over the seeds.

Tamping down the soil gently over the seeds serves two

purposes, first to hold down the seeds and second, to compact the soil particles just enough so that the capillary action in the soil will bring moisture to surround the seed. This is the opposite of the dust mulch principle, where the soil particles are broken up into a light fluffy mulch which will prevent soil moisture from being evaporated from the surface after the capillary action has brought it up from the depths of the top soil.

Certain seeds germinate so slowly that the rows should be marked with a faster germinating seed like radish. Some of the slow germinating seeds are parsley, carrots, leeks. These are all tiny seeds and should be sown in the furrow first. If you are using a rotary seeder which can be set to let the seed out at intervals, it will have to be reset for radish seed. The furrow is then covered with a thin layer of fine compost and is filled in and patted down. The radish seedlings will come up first, identifying the location of the row until the tinier seedlings also appear.

### Two Hours to Sow the Spring Garden

According to actual records kept year after year, it takes about two hours to sow an average of twenty rows, each about fifteen feet long. This presupposes that all tools are on hand and in working condition before starting. Peas and onion sets require individual attention and are slow planting, but it is possible with a rotary seeder to sow seed as fast as one can walk the length of the row. The rotary seeder also makes it possible to sow the row without stooping. Two persons can plant in slightly less time because one can stay at each end of the row to move the marking strings, and there is less need of walking back and forth.

### Plant Peas and Onion Sets as Early as Possible — and Garlic Even Earlier!

Peas and onion sets can be sown as early in the spring as you can walk into the garden without the soil sticking to your boots. Garlic cloves (single flat-sided bulbs broken or cleft off the larger bud of garlic) should be inserted into the soil at the earliest possible moment. The same early moisture which makes the mud also helps insure a good crop of peas. We have planted peas among ice crystals in the soil, but peas are so hardy that the cold does not harm them unless they are sown so deep that they rot in the furrows. Onion sets, which are tiny onions grown the previous year from seed, are also hardy enough to stand almost any amount of cold, or even snow. It may be noticed, however, that seeds sown a week or two later, if they get adequate moisture, will catch up with the earlier plantings. It is important to learn which vegetables are hardy and which seeds are tender, and to plant them accordingly.

## Make the Rows Short

For the gardener whose time is limited, there is more incentive to plant and care for three fifteen-foot rows of vegetables than one row forty-five feet long. It is also easier to keep shorter rows straight. Later in the season when weeds become a problem, it is simpler to keep them under control if the rows are shorter and therefore quicker to weed. We have found that the Bio-Dynamic raised beds about three and one-half feet wide by about fifteen feet long are an ideal size for planting and for weeding. (These raised beds may also be fitted in among other row crops in the garden.) One can reach halfway across the bed from either side, so there is no spot that is hard to reach. One can sit in the middle of the raised bed and reach at least one-third of the entire bed; thus one can weed the entire bed, only changing one's position twice.

As mentioned above, the first year these beds should be carefully laid out with stakes and string and then hoed up from the pathways alongside the beds. After the first year, the beds will still hold their shape and will need no other preparation than a sprinkling of compost, slight hoeing or raking to raise them up again, and then sowing. It is also quite practical to prepare and sow one bed at a time, thus reducing considerably the time spent in early spring sowing, and the time spent in planning and sowing successive crops later in the season.

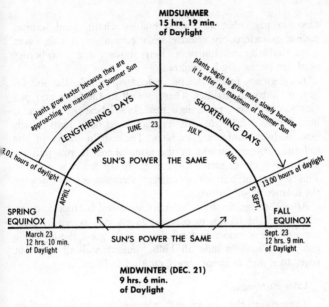

MIDSUMMER
15 hrs. 19 min.
of Daylight

plants grow faster because they are approaching the maximum of Summer Sun

plants begin to grow more slowly because it is after the maximum of Summer Sun

LENGTHENING DAYS

SHORTENING DAYS

JUNE 23

MAY

JULY

AUG.

SUN'S POWER THE SAME

3.01 hours of daylight

13.00 hours of daylight

APRIL 7

5 SEPT.

SPRING
EQUINOX

FALL
EQUINOX

March 23
12 hrs. 10 min.
of Daylight

SUN'S POWER THE SAME

Sept. 23
12 hrs. 9 min.
of Daylight

MIDWINTER (DEC. 21)
9 hrs. 6 min.
of Daylight

Figure 6.

# Crop Rotation

Since various vegetables make quite specific demands on soil nutrients, it is important in sowing the garden to follow a careful system of crop rotation. This is hard to specify exactly, but we can give the general rules here and let each gardener work out his own crop rotation with special regard to his individual situation and plants.

Heavy feeders need a heavy fertilizing with manure if possible. These should be followed by legumes which restore soil fertility. The third planting should be composed of light feeders or compost lovers, which should be fertilized with a good Bio-Dynamic compost. The heavy feeders are: cabbage, cauliflower in particular, all leaf vegetables: chard, head lettuce, endive, spinach, celery, celeriac, leeks, cucumbers, squash, sweet corn, rhubarb, and tomatoes. Berry bushes and strawberries need rich but not fresh manure.

The legumes follow the heavy feeders, to help the soil regain its nutrient qualities. These are all in the bean and pea family: pole beans, peas, sugar peas, broad beans, shell beans, lima beans, soya beans. All legumes have deep roots which bear nodules containing bacteria. These help to fix in the soil the nitrogen present in the atmosphere. If you pull up a bean or a clover plant, you can easily see the root nodules. This is part of nature's wonderful arrangement to preserve the balance of soil fertility.

After the legumes have helped restore soil balance and fertility, the light feeders or compost lovers may be sown. They require only a moderate fertilizing with a good Bio-Dynamic compost. These include all bulbs, onions and all the root vegetables, such as carrots, beets, radishes and turnips.

### Later Plantings

Throughout the spring and summer, successive plantings will need to be made. Only the hardy seeds can go in in the early spring; later it will be warm enough for the half-hardy sowings and for second sowings of such important items as lettuce and spinach. Experience teaches one how much of each vegetable to sow at one time. For instance, if one sows too much lettuce at one time, it all matures at once and there is more than the family can eat. Therefore it is better to make successive sowings two weeks apart. It is also well to experiment with different varieties of lettuce because some will withstand the hot weather in midsummer. We have had good success sowing a summer variety such as Oak Leaf in midsummer when it got a good start, and then grew larger tender heads as the weather grew cooler in the fall.

Green beans will mature in midsummer in about six weeks — our shortest crop. It is especially necessary to make successive sowings of green beans to extend the season over a long period.

As the season progresses and finally wanes after the warmest part of July, and the days grow shorter, vegetables which grew faster before midsummer now show a noticeable delay in maturing. On the other hand, plants which do not thrive under the hot summer sun, will begin to pick up and grow again as the heat subsides and the nights grow cool. The moist weather in the fall will bring to life many dormant plants that had looked dead.

For these reasons, the garden should be planned to include a growing season in late summer and early fall when lettuces, carrots, spinach, cabbage and especially broccoli and Brussels sprouts can be carried along until frost. Someone who has had wide experience writes: "I usually get my best broccoli after cold weather." This automatically gets around the worst criticism of broccoli: the tiny green worms that are so active in warm weather. If the broccoli matures long after the green worm season, you will never see a green worm because they just aren't there.

## Care of the Garden

### Cultivation

If your garden was spaded in the fall, it will not have to be respaded in the spring. It should be raked or criled and planted immediately.

If the weather is favorable, everything should be carried out in rapidly succeeding operations in one day:

raking or cultivating the soil
staking out the beds
making the seed furrows
sowing the seed
covering the furrows with good Bio-Dynamic compost
firming the seeds so they will not lie too loose and so
    that they will get enough moisture for germination

It is better to complete one small piece of garden land in a day than to spade up a large area and let it lie open to the sun and the wind. The process of raking or criling breaks up lumps which might otherwise dry and harden. All seeds prefer a freshly prepared soil, and no subsequent watering can replace the original moisture in the soil in the early spring. One of the principles of Bio-Dynamic gardening is to be careful not to leave the soil open or uncovered for any length of time. Uncovered soil is like a wound in the skin of the earth, and it should be covered or protected by mulch.

### Watering

Many amateur gardeners become alarmed when they see the leaves of their vegetables or flowers wilting in the hot summer sun. They run to get the hose, thinking the plants are wilting because they lack moisture. Actually the plant deliberately lets its leaves droop to prevent the hot sun from drawing the moisture from the flat leaf surface. Unless there is something else the matter — like bacterial wilt or a borer — the squash vine which was wilted and tired-looking in the afternoon, will be fresh and crisp the next morning.

However, there are times when one should water. But do not water, particularly over a heavy soil, unless it is really necessary. The need for water should be controlled by other measures such as hoeing, hilling and mulching. If watering is then necessary, the water to be used should, if possible, have stood for a time in the sun and the air. Rainwater is best of all, because it contains elements brought in from the outer air.

It is better to water seldom and thoroughly than frequently and superficially. Otherwise the pampered plants develop only shallow, sprawling roots. Then too, if water is once omitted, they suffer more than plants which have learned to push their roots to deeper soil levels in search of water. In hot, dry periods the garden should be divided into quarters. Perhaps once or twice weekly, according to need, each quarter should receive its generous share of water. The worried gardener need not wear himself out carrying a watering can, although he must certainly water fresh sowings and transplants, young seedlings and some especially thirsty plants, such as radishes and lettuce, every day. Cold spraying with a hose under great pressure should always be avoided, as well as watering in full sunlight. During the spring and fall when the nights are cool, it is preferable to water in the morning. In the summertime, when the danger of chilling the soil and plants is past, watering in order to freshen the plants should be done in the evening. It is a general principle of plant hygiene that if the soil (and this applies to houseplants in pots, too) is kept on the dry side when there is danger of chilling, the plant will survive the cold better. If the soil is saturated with water, the latter is a conductor of the cold, and the roots are likely to be chilled.

### Hoeing

Immediately after the seedlings have sprouted and the seed leaves have appeared, hoeing or cultivation should begin. For seeds which germinate slowly, a marking seed like radish will make the row visible early. The gardener should keep in mind that soil moisture is never still: it is either falling as rain or rising through capillary attraction to evaporate at the surface of the soil. The impacted soil particles in the top crust (impacted by raindrops or footprints) enable the moisture to evaporate quickly, and therefore the crust must be broken up with a hoe or rake or similar tool. The broken crust thus forms a dust mulch which checks evaporation on the surface.

Three things are achieved by hoeing:

1. breaking the crust so the soil moisture cannot travel upwards;
2. aeration of the top crust and
3. the destruction of tiny weed seedlings which are easily hoed up at this stage.

When the seedling roots are still very small and delicate, hoeing should be very gentle and shallow. Later, after the plants have sent strong roots down to deeper levels, it is safe to hoe more deeply. If the surface of the garden is kept well hoed, with a good "dust mulch," less watering will be required.

It is of importance to hoe over the surface lightly at exactly the right moment after each rainstorm: that is, when the soil is just dried out enough to support your footsteps without picking up mud on your shoes. The soil should be as damp as possible, but not wet. The dampness in the soil makes it delightful to work with the hoe, and the whole garden may be hoed over very quickly. This is also the time to pull weeds whose roots, loosened by the rain, let go easily with a slight pull. These subtle changes in moisture and temperature are only noticed by the gardener who spends time in quiet contemplation and "feeling" in his garden. As one friend has written, "I still believe that an hour spent leaning on a hoe may do more good than thrashing around in the garden in an aimless way." ["Seven Years of B.D. Gardening," Arnold C. Brugger, BIO-DYNAMICS, No. 58 Spring 1961, p. 19.]

Cultivation with the hoe takes care of the tiny weeds. Especially at the beginning of the season, until the vegetables get a real start, all the weeds should be removed by cultivation with a crile, hoe, wheel hoe, or any other tool that is congenial to use. If the garden soil is broken over the surface with a hoe about once a week, the little weed seedlings will cause no trouble. A weed seed can sprout only once. If the seedling is cut off at the base when it is young, it cannot grow again. The time to exterminate weeds is early, when they are young and tender, not in the middle of the summer when they have grown tough woody stalks and deep roots. Chemical weed killers are never used in the Bio-Dynamic garden. They are dangerous to use and they are unnecessary when weeds can be so easily hoed out. Furthermore, the promiscuous use of chemicals upsets the balance of natural forces, and no one knows what damage may be done.

After the vegetables (and flowers, I hope!) are well established, it is permissible to let a few weeds grow around the edges of the garden to provide protection from the wind and to give a little shade. Some weeds have a beneficial effect upon garden plants. The good influence of weeds is the subject of several books. Yarrow and dandelion help neighboring plants. Lamb's quarter is another weed which apparently does no harm to its neighbors and does supply an edible green, both in early spring when the whole plant can be eaten, and later in the summer when the tender green tips and leaves are edible and delicious.

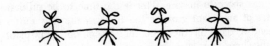

Plants growing on sparse soil are small
but strongly aromatic in essential oils.

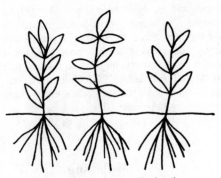

Plants growing on rich, deep, fertile soil
are large and fleshy with a bland flavor.

**Figure 7.**

Some Bio-Dynamic gardeners make a practice of hilling all kinds of garden vegetables in order to give them firmer hold in the earth. Hilling in this case means simply hoeing up a small mound of soil around the stem of the plant. It is well to apply compost or well rotted manure before hilling. When leeks are hilled, the result is a beautifully blanched stem. Tomatoes, when hilled, send out rootlets from their stems and so increase their root capacity. Everyone, of course, hills potatoes.

This section cannot be left without special mention of thinning out the extra seedlings in every row, sometimes with the hoe and sometimes by hand. Probably the hardest part of gardening is to destroy the perfect little seedlings that grew too thick in the row. When a seedling is half an inch across, it is hard to believe it will require six to twelve inches of row space to mature. This is the time to be ruthless. Seedlings of any plant growing too thick in the row are no better than weeds. Pull them up, hoe them out, transplant them somewhere else, give them away, do anything, but give your chosen plants plenty of space! Few of us realize that although a carrot is only one or two inches in diameter as it appears in the row, its tiny feeder roots extend in a circle five feet in diameter and go down to a depth of eight feet by actual measurement. No wonder carrots are stunted if they grow too close together! Some vegetables like carrots may be thinned out during the growing season, providing the family table with tender young carrots, meanwhile making room for others to grow to full size before fall. Onion sets can be planted every two inches and thinned, since every other one is big enough to use on the dinner table.

## Mulching

After the garden is weeded and thinned and hoed and hilled, it may also be mulched. A mulch is a thick layer of protective material spread over the soil, between the plants for two purposes: nourishment and protection against loss of moisture.

A mulch for nourishment may be made of unfinished compost, the fibrous content of roots, straw, leaves, or half-rotted leaf mold, or weeds which were cut before they had time to go to seed. Grass clippings may be used for a mulch but should be watched because they heat up and may burn the plants underneath.

A mulch for protection to prevent evaporation of soil moisture should be applied when the ground is moist. This should be carefully watched and removed during a rainy period, otherwise the soil underneath may be waterlogged and may become acid and unhealthy. If the mulch is put on as a protection against weeds, it should be so thick the weeds cannot penetrate, or will be so weak that they can easily be pulled up by hand. A layer of straw or leaves at least two inches thick will achieve this weed protection.

Mulches may be made of almost any material laid over the soil: weeds, straw, hay, leaves, polyethelene plastic, even stones. There are machines for mixing a mulch of paper, garbage and compost in equal quantities. This was a very satisfactory material which provided a good soil cover and attracted the earthworms. The only drawback was that it was difficult to make enough to cover large spaces between the plants.

Mulching should never be used without a careful study of the soil because different kinds of soil require different treatment. A sandy soil is benefited especially by a mulch. Sometimes the only way to make a heavy clay soil crumbly is to mulch it. There are several dangers to be avoided. For instance, the soil underneath the mulch may become waterlogged. Orchards may develop serious fungus diseases in such cases. A moldy mulch will create an acid soil which prevents assimilation of nitrogen. If the mulch keeps the soil waterlogged through the winter, plants may be heaved out by the frost. Pests of many kinds are very happy to hibernate in a mulch cover: mice, rats and rabbits will do irreparable damage to young fruit trees if the mulch comes too close to the tree trunks. A dry mulch may also become a fire hazard.

Some people, from an aesthetic standpoint, object to the appearance of a layer of mulching materials. While garden plants look beautiful growing out of a rich brown soil, they look grotesquely choked when surrounded by a thick mulch of hay. Furthermore, if the hay or straw has not been thoroughly thrashed, one may succeed in sowing a hayfield all over one's vegetable garden! A mulch of prepared and marketed materials such as buckwheat hulls or peat moss is very expensive.

Recent experiments with the Bio-Dynamic Tree Paste show some promise that it can be used for mulch, sprayed on the soil between the rows of plants. Grapevines, cane and bush berries and strawberries are all benefited by some kind of mulch.

Snow is a good mulch, provided in lavish quantities, free of charge! In a lecture on Bio-Dynamic practices in the garden, Dr. E. E. Pfeiffer once made these comments: "Mulch does the same thing that snow does: it warms the soil to the same depth as the height of the mulch. If there is a three-foot snowfall, the effect of the snow reaches down into the soil to a depth of three feet. A mulch acts in the same way. It holds moisture, makes the structure crumbly and encourages the biological processes as deep in the ground as the thickness of the cover. In a heavy, sticky clay soil, build the mulch up to one or two feet and just let it lie there. It should, however, be carefully checked. If put on when the soil is too dry, it will prevent rain from penetrating. The mice, beetles and insects will hibernate there. Remove the mulch to aerate the soil and replace with new material. If it is perforated by many little holes you may find many borers and bettles are being protected there.

"The winter moisture and frost ought to be allowed to penetrate the soil to help the formation of a beneficial structure. The mulch may have to be removed to let air and frost into the soil. When to put the mulch back on will depend on the moisture content of the soil."

## Fall Cultivation

Fall cultivation has many advantages. The man with the plow has less pressure from immediate tasks and he can plow the garden almost any time before frost. Fall plowing encourages the penetration of winter cold and moisture. The soil should be plowed, but not deep enough to bring up the subsoil, and left in clods for the frost to freeze and the sun to thaw throughout the winter. Even a heavy clay soil that has been plowed and left rough in the fall will be ready for planting the next spring, with only a thorough raking to smooth out the lumps. Once the organic humus structure is established, there will be little danger of soil erosion because of fall plowing. Of course, one should be careful to plow on the contour when first plowing on a sloping area. Protective hedgerows also should be used whenever possible to prevent wind

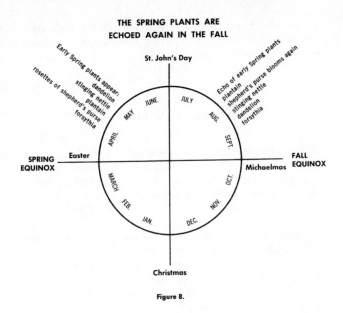

**THE SPRING PLANTS ARE
ECHOED AGAIN IN THE FALL**

St. John's Day

Early Spring plants appear:
dandelion
stinging nettle
plantain
rosettes of shepherd's purse
forsythia

Echo of early Spring plants:
plantain
shepherd's purse blooms again
stinging nettle
dandelion
forsythia

JUNE    JULY

MAY     AUG.

APRIL   SEPT.

**SPRING
EQUINOX**    Easter

Michaelmas    **FALL
EQUINOX**

MARCH   OCT.

FEB.    NOV.

JAN.    DEC.

Christmas

Figure 8.

erosion after fall plowing. Most backyard gardens are too small to require extensive contour plowing or windbreaks, but even the backyard gardener should utilize these principles if he can.

In a new garden area which is still in sod, instead of turning the sods under, the ground may be thickly "peeled" with a hoe or a mattock, and the weeds should be put into the compost heap. If the green weeds are left in the earth to decompose, they will attract wire worms and other soil pests. The sods that were peeled off should be made into compost which will be of superior quality if it is interlayered with cow manure. Removing sods will help uncover and bring to light the grub stage of the June beetle and other insects.

If you intend only to spade, this also should be done in the fall if possible. All the garden beds should lie in rough clods

70

over the winter, except of course, those planted with vegetables to be wintered over (parsnips, perennial onions, horse
radish, rhubarb, and the perennial herbs).

## Insect Pests

When a Bio-Dynamic gardener sets out to control an infestation of insects, instead of reaching for a bug-bomb to anni-
hilate, he tries first to figure out the cause of the infestation.
What can I learn from the presence of these insects? Is there
some imbalance in my garden which makes it suddenly attractive to them?

He goes on to question: Is there too much or too little moisture, sunlight, soil aeration, compost, shade, mulch, cultivation? — and so on? What insect is it, and what are the various
stages of its life cycle? What are its characteristics? What does
it like? What does it dislike? Is there some mechanical method for dislodging the insects? — or trapping them? — or
keeping them out — or driving them away?

EXAMPLES: A soft brush or cold water will wash away
aphids. A stream of cold air will keep house
flies out.
Shaking will dislodge the curculio beetles from
apple trees.

What are the natural enemies of this insect in his present stage,
in his larval stage, and in his egg stage?

EXAMPLES: The list of insectivorous creatures is encyclo-
pedic: birds, moles, toads, spiders, snakes, and
so on.

Finally, if all these considerations do not keep the insects at
least under control, the next — and last step — is to search
for a harmless material which will either drive the insects away
or destroy them without harming other beneficial things in their
environment. For example: moths are repelled by camphor,
tar or aromatic herbs which cannot harm anything nearby.

71

Therefore, plant sage or tansy which are both high in camphor content, close to fruit trees which are bothered by the coddling moth.

Again we would emphasize that the practice of Bio-Dynamics, especially in one's own garden is a close study of subtle processes rather than the application of a series of definite recipes. It makes only a slight difference whether one uses a poisonous chemical or an equally poisonous botanical to kill the garden insects. The latter may do as much damage as the former in the way of widespread killing of the insect life and damage to living soil bacteria. We therefore prefer not to use any kind of poisons in the garden, but to control insect invasions by first destroying egg clusters before they hatch, hand picking adult insects, and then watching closely for any larvae which may have hatched from undetected eggs. We also try to keep the whole garden area well filled with aromatic herbs and substances which we know to be insect-repellent.

However, none of these methods is one hundred per cent effective, because of the changing, dynamic element among living things. What serves to repel an insect at one season may fail woefully six weeks later. For instance, we notice every summer that the cabbage butterfly is repelled by the onions only during the early part of June. Later, the cabbage butterfly lays her eggs regardless of onions or other strong herbs nearby. Another example of the apparent failure of these old-time remedies: for several years potato bugs have been less sensitive to the repellent effect of bush beans in some places. Subtle changes may be taking place in either the potato bugs or in the plants, or perhaps in rainfall or in temperature, and it will take years of close observation and experience to learn what is causing these changes. We cannot honestly, from our own experience, make extravagant claims to infallible successes with biological controls, although we have certainly tried for many years to prove them.

The following is a brief outline taken from recent issues of BIO-DYNAMICS giving some highlights of controls of common insect pests which have worked in some places at some times. We have tried as far as possible to locate and study examples of all these dynamic influences between growing plants

## Companion Plants in a Biodynamic Garden

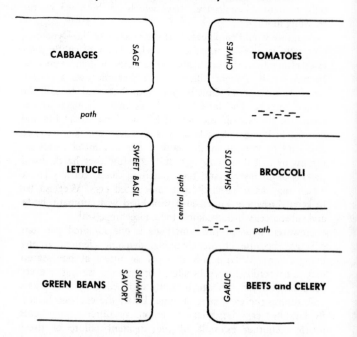

These and many other combinations improve
the health of the garden and of the consumers.

**Figure 9.**

and living insects and their biological controls. Experience
and observation teach us that biological balances are badly up-
set by external influences these days so that many old-time remedies are not as effective as some claim them to be:

Japanese Beetles may be controlled by the use of Bug
Doom, or milky spore disease, put out by Fairfax Biological
Laboratory, Clinton Corners, New York. Some communities
distribute this material free to their inhabitants and thus bring

73

the Japanese Beetle under control. This is an outstandingly successful example of biological control.

For mosquito control try goldfish. Dragon Flies also devour mosquitoes. The Lace Wing Fly and its larvae eat caterpillar eggs, mites in all stages, scale insects, aphids and mealy bugs. The lady bug and its larvae eat aphids and scale insects. The Syrphid Fly and its larvae eat aphids. Female wasps lay their eggs in the larvae of caterpillars and other harmful insects. When the wasp larvae hatch, they devour the host larvae. Obnoxious insects of many kinds are controlled by ground beetles, tiger beetles, preying mantis, robber flies and spiders. They are also eaten by small animals and reptiles: shrews, skunks, bats, snakes, newts, toads, lizards.

Electric Insect Traps (Detjen Corporation, Pleasant Valley, New York) have been used to control beetles: curculio, fire-flies, Japanese beetles, May and June beetles, click beetles; moths: coddling moth, tent caterpillar, corn earworm and corn borer; flies: mosquitoes, house flies and barn flies.

Dr. Pfeiffer once told of visiting an orchard where the ground under the trees was covered with a sheet, and the curculio were shaken down several days in succession onto the sheet, whence they were gathered up and destroyed.

There is no substitute for constant study of actual conditions in one's own garden, including close observation and frequent expeditions with magnifying glass and flashlight to see what goes on at night as well as in the daylight. The night flying insects are entirely different from those to be found in the daytime.

## Companion Plants

One of the chief differences between Bio-Dynamics and other organic methods of gardening is that Bio-Dynamics makes use of the dynamic effects of living things acting upon each other. The dynamic effects are always there, but Bio-Dynamics makes a conscious effort to study, to harness the forces and to use them in the growth processes. A living plant at noonday has qualities which differ from those it had at sunrise of the same day. At evening it will be still different.

By careful observation and study through the years, people have learned that different kinds of plants, growing close together, have certain effects upon each other. Sometimes these effects are mutually beneficial, sometimes detrimental. For instance, one summer we had fairly good sunflowers but very poor potatoes. Later we learned that these two plants always have an unfortunate effect on one another.

This study goes on continuuusly, and the effort is to learn how to make use of these mutually beneficial effects so that we can grow superior produce in our backyard gardens. The results show in finer flavor and better keeping qualities, as well as in high nutritional qualities which can now be tested by chromatograms in the laboratory.

The amateur gardener, learning about companion plants and mixed cultures for the first time, would do well to follow the rules exactly until he has gained experience and knowledge of the qualities of various plants. The rules are based on many years of observation and experience. One example might be cited of a gardener who heard that bush beans would repel Colorado potato beetles. Later in the season when the Colorado potato beetles were moving into his garden in hordes, an investigation was made and it turned out that he had planted lima beans with his potatoes. To a casual observer it would seem that bush beans (usually meaning green snap beans) and limas, both being legumes, would act in the same way. Evidently the Colorado potato beetle is not a casual observer!

There are many different aspects to be considered in mixed cultures and companion plants, and one of these is that shallow rooting and deep rooting plants supplement each other. With their deep roots legumes aerate the soil and promote root growth in their neighbors. A tall, thin plant supplements the low bush plant: the long, slender leek likes to grow near the stocky celeriac plant. Both like potassium and do well if they can be fertilized with well-rotted pig manure.

Short season plants like the kohlrabi, which matures early and is harvested, supplement slower growing plants, leaving room for the slower growing beets to expand into the space thus left open.

If someone were to ask what we like best about Bio-Dynamic gardening, we would say "Companion Plants!" Because these plant species like each other, they both do well in each other's company, and over the whole garden there hovers a feeling of contentment: the green beans and the strawberries like to grow together, and each bears better fruit because of the other. The green peas provide the nitrogen the spinach uses, and the peas, in turn are benefited by the carrots growing nearby. All the smaller plants enjoy the tall protection of the pole beans and their leguminous contributions to the soil, while the herbs pour out their aroma and fragrance into an atmosphere congenial to the more stolid vegetables. Thus, sage and thyme and oregano and rosemary uplift and enliven the lumpy cabbage and help to create a fine balance in the garden.

The list of congenial companion plants is long and varied. It has given some of us a special project for many years to isolate and try out each combination, one by one. Instead of trying to list all combinations here, we would refer the reader to the booklet titled COMPANION PLANTS by Richard Gregg. This has become a classic for the Bio-Dynamic gardener, for it contains enough information for a lifetime of study and experiment. It is a masterful assemblage of Bio-Dynamic discoveries which cannot be too highly recommended.

## Edible Wild Plants

It is hardly fair to confine our approach to those edible plants which are raised in the garden when so many edible plants grow wild all around us. Numerous books have been written on this subject. PLANTS FOR SURVIVAL is the title of a recently published outline by the Armed Services. It tells how to find edible plants on which to survive if one is cast ashore in various parts of the world.

Some of the common weeds which we remove from the

vegetable garden can also be used for food, but it is quite necessary to make sure of the identity of the plant before eating it. The botanical name helps to make identification accurate.

A combination of spring greens may include all or any of the following plants, gathered while they are still very small and tender:

Stinging Nettle (*Urtica dioica*) not over 3"-4" high
Dandelion (*Taraxacum officinale*) before buds form
Poke Weed (*Phytolacca americana*) only until flower buds appear (Poke Weed is poisonous if eaten too late in the season.)
Lamb's Quarter or Smooth Pigweed (*Chenopodium album*)
Dock (*Rumex crispus*)
Wild Lettuce (*Latuca elongata*)
Blue Stem, or Salt and Pepper
Pink Root or Amaranthus

Fiddle Heads, the early fronds of Bracken, and other ferns may be cooked like asparagus after being cleaned of the hairy fuzz which keeps them warm in early spring. They should be tied in bunches and steamed. They can even be canned with the pressure cooker.

Other wild plants furnish salad material in the colder parts of the year, before the garden season in spring or after the fall harvest. The blossoms of the Red Bud Tree, sometimes called "Salad Tree" can be gathered and eaten. Green elm seeds are high in flavor and nutrition. Wild mustard, wild lettuce, and the tender leaves of dandelion and chicory, as well as tender tips of alfalfa can be added to salads. Saint Barbara's Cress may be used in small quantities for a winter salad since it stays green and crisp even under the snow. Very young leaves of horse radish are also an addition to salads.

Late spring greens may be enjoyed in the Milk Weed plant shoots, before it grows tough and flannelly. Summer salads and greens can be enhanced by the refreshing and slightly acid taste of Purslane (*Portulaca oleracea*) which can be cooked like spinach or eaten raw in salad.

Other parts of these plants may be used in addition to the

leaves. The roots of chicory and dandelion may be dried, ground, and used for coffee. The root of the horseradish may be washed, cut in smallish pieces, added to a little vinegar in an electric blender and chopped until it is a smooth paste.

Cookbooks of olden times even included Tansy Pudding!

## Harvesting, Cooking and Preserving

The rule, briefly, for harvesting produce from the Bio-Dynamic garden is to pick the vegetables before they are mature. Be very careful to keep them shaded from the hot sun as they are being harvested. We usually carry a large basket with a big rhubarb leaf or a thick cabbage leaf to shade the basket. Some say the pot should be boiling before you start toward the garden!

The compost heap near the garden makes an ideal place to prepare the vegetables, as you cut off outer leaves before they go into the house. The leaves and other waste parts, of course, are added directly to the compost.

In the kitchen the rule is, the less cooking, the better — in the minimum amount of water — but this is a very broad subject with many shades of opinion!

Most people agree that freezing is preferable to canning if fruits and vegetables have to be preserved. The necessity for long sterilization in canning takes some of the goodness out of home grown produce. Freezing, however, seems to do a minimum of harm to flavor and texture and we recommend a home deep-freezer because of its constant convenience.

While we are on the subject of freezing, it might be well to suggest that people make their own experiments in freezing without blanching. Government bulletins and cookbooks recommend blanching in boilding water for a few seconds or over steam to inhibit the enzymatic action in the vegetables. It has been our experience, however, that if vegetables are gathered when slightly immature, and are rushed directly into the deep freeze, they can be frozen satisfactorily without first blanching. (All herbs and most vegetables should be carefully harvested before ten o'clock in the morning because their aromatic qualities evaporate later in the day.) Another shortcut we have found practical is to spread the vegetables to be frozen on a cloth placed directly on the bottom of the freezing compartment so they will freeze very quickly. As soon as the pieces are frozen solid, lift the cloth and the frozen pieces will tumble into freezer packages, practically packing themselves. When the product is needed for the table, it is possible to shake out half or three-quarters of the contents which did not freeze together in a chunk, as they do if blanched and then packed.

We would also encourage people to make their own experiments with freezing all kinds of garden produce. It takes very little time and trouble to fill a few packages, just to see what can be frozen. Printed matter on this subject is noticeably conservative. Most books say tomatoes cannot be frozen, but a friend of ours skins them and cuts them into quarters before freezing. When thawed there is more juice than pulp, but it has a fresh, uncooked flavor. Government bulletins say that none of the leafy vegetables will stand freezing because the tissues are injured and become stringy and wilted. However, we have had good success freezing Kale and shredded cabbage, spinach and lamb's quarter, milkweed, and mixed greens. Summer squash freezes better if partially cooked, and so do parsnips, beets and Brussels sprouts. This is another subject too broad to be handled here, and the reader is advised to make a special study of the books available on the subject.

Anyone fortunate enough to have a cold storage space in a cellar where vegetables will not freeze, is indeed lucky. Root vegetables of all kinds, stored in crocks with an uncorked bottle of water, will keep perfectly fresh and firm until the following spring. Here are some rules: Don't store apples near anything else, because the apples give off ethylyne gas and make other things ripen. Keep apples away from carrots. Keep potatoes away from apples, or the apples will taste like the potatoes.

# Saving Seeds

Many Bio-Dynamic gardeners save their seeds and use them year after year. Some of these seeds are especially good because they have been acclimatized to local weather conditions and to the soil where they grew. If they were saved from the best plants in the garden with careful, experienced attention, they are well worth planting. If, however, they are gathered at random they may not be worth planting. Seed selection is a technical job, requiring special training and experience in observation of the plant whose traits one wishes to perpetutate. The seeds themselves look good and may come from fine fruit, but that does not insure that they will be suitable in every climate. The cantaloupe whose seeds look so good may have grown in the south where the season is long and temperate. Some fruit cannot be grown from seeds, but is better started from slips or plants. Some plants even revert to the color and size of their original species when the seeds are saved year after year: witness the uninteresting mauve petunia or phlox which hang on year after year unless new seed or new plants are imported to improve the color.

Seed brought in from a neighbor's garden may also carry plant diseases such as smuts or rusts. People who know, recommend that amateurs should play with home-grown seeds if they like, but they should not plan to feed the family with the resulting crop! It goes without saying that seeds from hybrid crops should never be saved because they will not grow true to type the following year.

If, after all this warning, you still want to save your own seed, this is how to do it: Observe carefully which plant is the healthiest, or the earliest to fruit, or the sturdiest, or the most resistant to disease. Save the best fruit from this plant. "Cucumbers and tomatoes must go through a little extra process of fermentation. Pick the fruits just before they are dead ripe, set them out on a plate in a shady place until they get squashy. Scrape the seeds and pulp out onto a shallow dish or plate, add a little water, and let ferment for forty-eight hours. You can tell that they are fermenting by the little bubbles that form in the water. Then put the mass in a sieve and wash the pulp off under the cold water faucet. Spread the cleaned seeds out on blotting paper in the shade to dry. Once they are completely dry, put them in an envelope and store. Squash, pepper and eggplant seed is treated similarly." (BIODYNAMICS VII No. 4. p. 33)

Seeds are so full of life that they are especially attractive to mice — who really know what is good to eat. If you are not vigilant, you may find the mouse has found your seed supply while you were waiting for it to ferment. Several people have told about seeds left to dry, which were quite safe for several weeks until suddenly one night the mice ate every one!

# Herbs

Each year various garden clubs and herb societies seem to rediscover facts about herbs which Bio-Dynamic gardeners have been using in their gardens for years. In addition to many indispensible uses for cooking, for perfumes and for simple home remedies, herbs are most useful in the garden while they are growing with other plants. The chapter on COMPANION PLANTS enumerates some of these dynamic effects. We have already touched upon biological control of insects, which is also suggested in the section on insect pests, where some of our finest culinary herbs and salad plants do double duty in warding off some common garden pests.

Any library or bookshop will offer a generous supply of herb books. Most herbs are not difficult to raise and will respond happily to cultivation according to the simple rules explained in any book. Once you commence to experiment with herbs in your garden, you are assured many happy experiences and fascinating hours as well as a Bio-Dynamic garden of heightened health and activity. You will also find that the love of herbs brings together a most congenial host of friendly people with one interest in common.

# Lawns

Someone always asks anxiously, "What can I do for my lawn?" One answer is to remember that the main plant in the lawn is grass, which likes cool weather and thrives in spring and early summer, but which naturally turns brown in hot, dry weather. We have found that grass and clover in the lawn respond to application of Bio-Dynamic compost at the same rate as the garden: 1 pint or 1 pound to every two square feet. As the nitrogen increases in the soil, from the presence of the clover, the grass will increase until there is too much nitrogen. Then the grass will take over, enjoying the nitrogen, and the clover will decrease. This balancing action will go on indefinitely if the lawn is well fertilized. As for dandelions, dig them out and eat them if they offend. Otherwise let them grow to improve the health of the surrounding grass. Contrary to idle comment, dandelions will never take over a lawn entirely. The lawn may be "just golden with blossoms" for a few days in the spring, but they soon blow away — literally!

# Flowers

We have purposely not mentioned flowers in this treatment of the Bio-Dynamic garden because it is understood that one just naturally sprinkles flowering plants all over the garden, wherever there is space. Sometimes we have grown a different flower at the foot of each raised bed to balance the herbs at the head of each bed. If one has a love for growing plants, there will be no problem in finding places for flowers which add so much in color and beauty and in attracting the beneficial honey bees and butterflies to the garden. It might be added here that a few spring bulbs should be set out for their early spring charm, and also to serve as a natural thermometer to tell when to plant the garden in the early spring.

# The Home Orchard

Home raising of fruits has become practically a necessity in these days of heavily sprayed commercial fruits, but this is too long a subject for this study. Dr. E. E. Pfeiffer has written a pamplet titled THE BIO-DYNAMIC TREATMENT OF FRUIT TREES, BERRIES AND SHRUBS, which is now available. This gives a complete picture of the cultural habits and needs of fruit trees, bushes and vines, with some explanation of the Bio-Dynamic point of view and up to date descriptions on how to treat fruit trees in order to get the best quality fruit from your Bio-Dynamic orchard, for your family's use.

## Other Helpers in the Bio-Dynamic Garden and Orchard

BEES — No Bio-Dynamic garden or orchard is complete with out its own honey bees. Their presence does more for the surrounding area than pollination of the flowers. They foster growth by giving off "bee scent substance" — for want of a better name — in their flight. Their presence aids all the plants in the neighborhood. But this is a subject for many books, and the reader is advised to go to the library and look up books on beekeeping if he wants to keep bees. It is probably the most fascinating of all subjects, and happy indeed is the Bio-Dynamic gardener whose bees are at home in his back yard!

BIRDS — Instead of having to make an effort to attract wild birds, we notice the wild birds seek out the Bio-Dynamic garden and make themselves at home there. Year after year we have entertained hordes of wild birds, roosting in our trees, devouring the feed we put out in winter and living in our birdhouses in summer. They especially enjoy the rows of sunflowers we plant for their food in winter, and the fruit-bearing ornamental shrubs. They also seem to enjoy taking baths in the bird baths we fill with water for them. The sparrows take dust baths in the dry dust of the chicken run, fraternizing with the hens the while — and occasionally snitching their share of the hens' scratch grain!

Recent issues of BIO-DYNAMICS have contained many references to the usefulness of birds in combatting insects. Wild birds do useful service in controlling caterpillars; these they feed to their young in unbelievably large quantities. Even the unpopular English Sparrow is credited with saving a crop from infestation with alfalfa weevil. The equally maligned starling goes after the caterpillars of the brown tail and gypsy moth with a vengeance. Starlings also burrow into the soil to catch the grubs of the Japanese beetle. Hawks and owls carry on a continuous control of rats, mice, gophers and moles. The nuthatch and the downy woodpecker work on the coddling moth in our fruit trees. We know them all, and we give them full credit for the work they do right here in our garden. Anyone fortunate enough to have an American cuckoo nearby should find fewer tent caterpillars because of his efforts. We probably don't have the Cuckoo, but last year we had some vigilant birds who cleaned up a tentful of caterpillars which we left in an apple tree to see who would clean it out first. This is all too brief a mention of these most helpful friends who fly about us unnoticed and unthanked much of the time.

## Current Publications on Gardening

So many magazines are now appearing regularly on the newsstands that one can never lack for popular information about gardening. One should notice, however, that many of these magazines seem to have one main idea, and that is to sell agricultural chemicals. By all means use the gardening information if it suits you, but please notice that unless you are following Bio-Dynamic principles as set forth in the first chapter of this book, you are not entirely a Bio-Dynamic gardener.

We urge everyone to follow as closely as possible the techniques and principles explained in the Bio-Dynamic literature. As Dr. E. E. Pfeiffer points out, "The Bio-Dynamic Method goes hand in hand with a striving for better quality," and in the long run, what we do to the soil in our own backyard may become the pattern of an enlightened attitude toward agriculture on a much larger scale.

# Most Frequently Asked Questions

## 1. What Are the Advantages of Raised Beds in the Bio-Dynamic Garden?

1. better drainage of moisture

2. increased aeration of the beds

3. greater ease in marking the rows and scatching the furrows for planting. Once the beds are established, there is no need to lay out rows with stakes and strings.

4. better tomato crops. The tomato likes to grow every year in the same place, being fertilized with compost of its own stalks. One or two raised beds may be set aside every year as tomato beds.

5. and most important: increased growth activity on the surface of a slightly raised bed. As Rudolf Steiner once pointed out, "Whenever in any given locality you have a general level of niveau, separating what is above the earth from the interior, all that is raised above this normal level of the district will show a special tendency to life — a tendency to permeate itself with .... vitality. Hence you will find it easier to permeate ordinary inorganic mineral earth with fruitful humus-substance, or with any waste-product in process of decomposition — you will find it easier to do this efficiently if you erect mounds of earth, and permeate these with the said substance. For then the earthly material itself will tend to become inwardly alive — akin to the plant-nature."

## 2. How Do You Know When Compost is Ready to Use?

It is possible to send samples of compost to the biochemical laboratory to have an analysis made to determine the time of maximum value in the compost. But for the practical gardener's use, it is enough to observe some simple signs of the compost:

1. The heap will settle to one-third or one-quarter its original size.

2. Most of the layered materials will be so broken down that they are hardly recognizable. Straw and leaves may re-

tain their shape, but you can crumble them easily in your hand.

3. Most of the heap looks and smells like good topsoil or forest leafmould.

4. Probably earthworms will be present.

From experience we have learned that the sooner we open a compost heap and use it, the more benefit we get from it. If it is left too long, it returns to rich topsoil.

It is almost impossible to name a definite time limit for making compost, because of differences in materials used, in soil bacteria present, in temperature of the seasons involved. To test the compost, slice into the shady end of the heap, vertically with a shovel. Make another vertical cut with the shovel and let the slice fall forward. If it crumbles easily, even though you can see remnants of straw and grass and leaves, it is ready to use. Be sure to put some rough insulating material like leaves over the slice when you leave the compost, for it must be shaded and protected from the wind. You know how a loaf of bread dries out after the first slice has been cut off!

### 3. Can I Raise Fruit Without the Use of Poison Sprays?

This is a very technical subject and a complete answer would be too long to give here. The overall answer is "Yes, it is possible to raise fruit without the use of poison sprays." Within a period of five years we have restored the vitality of a dozen or more old fruit trees: apples, pears, cherries. We followed carefully the instructions for the use of Bio-Dynamic tree sprays (which differ completely from chemical poisons) and each year we have a larger crop of fruit to harvest, although the fruit is not yet perfect. On a former site we started with new fruit trees and protected them as they matured by the use of Bio-Dynamic tree spray. For four or five years we gathered mouthwatering harvests of peaches. For further information on this subject the pamphlet BIO-DYNAMIC TREATMENT OF FRUIT TREES, BERRIES AND SHRUBS by E. E. Pfeiffer is recommended. There are also many practical hints for helpful plant companions in Richard

# The steady yearly rhythm in the Plant World.

**IN WINTER**
Plant life contracts into the Earth,
old plants decay and become topsoil.
New life is contracted into the seeds.
Water is frozen in compact crystals.
The Sun is far away in the sky and all life
on Earth shrinks inward to resist the cold.

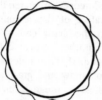

**IN SPRING**
The Sun returns and the Earth
relaxes. Water begins to rise in
the Plant World. Plants unfold
and begin to grow upward. Human
Beings come out of their
houses and begin to enjoy the
out of doors.

**IN SUMMER**
When the Sun is nearest the
Earth at midsummer, vegetable
life reaches its culmination.
The Earth is clothed in tall green
vegetation which is like fur
covering the surface of our planet.

**IN FALL**
The water in the plant world descends and
the plants lose their characteristic forms.
Tree leaves wither and shrivel. The Sun
draws further and further away—
but the seeds fall into the Earth bearing
promise of the return of Life next Spring.

Figure 10.

Gregg's pamphlet, COMPANION PLANTS. Complete information on the use of Biodynamic Tree Spray is available from Mr. Peter Escher, Threefold Farm, Spring Valley, New York.

#### 4. What About Japanese Beetles?

The Japanese Beetle can be brought under control by a white powder which is spores of the milky disease, which affects only the grubs of the Japanese Beetle. Research on milky spore disease was done by the United States Department of Agriculture and the facts are as follows: 10 ounces will treat about 2,500 square feet of lawn with viable spores of two kinds of bacilli. This powder has no effect whatever on beneficial insects, earthworms, plants, human beings, or warm blooded animals. One application is sufficient because the milky spore disease is transmitted by natural means to untreated areas. If everyone in a community would use this material, the Japanese Beetle could definitely be brought under control.

#### 5. What Should I Do for My Lawn?

For an old lawn, try a light sprinkling of good Bio-Dynamic compost and see how the growth improves. For a new planting, a lawn takes as thorough preparation as any seed bed: that is, deep cultivation and fertilizing with good compost, seeding, and watering with as much care as any garden.

Good results have also been obtained by the use of Bio-Dynamic bacterial starter sprinkled over the lawn in early spring. This works better if lawn clippings are always allowed to go back into the surface of the lawn after mowing. In other words, do not rake up the grass clippings.

#### 6. Is Anything Gained by Planning According to the Phases of the Moon?

An experienced gardener may observe some very amazing facts if he learns to watch the growth in his garden while he observes the phases of the moon. There are noticeable spurts of growth at certain times which coincide with the full moon and the dark of the moon, especially if the garden is kept well watered. On the other hand, during the periods between, growth is constant and not spectacular. If seeds can be sown to make the most of these increased growth periods, very encouraging results will be obtained. There is some dependable scientific literature on this subject, but it is too detailed to quote here. Future authoritative study of space and of the radiations from various planetary bodies will in time reveal the scientific reasons why the garden benefits by being planted during the right phases of the moon.

### 7. Should I Put Lime on My Garden?

Rather than put lime directly into the garden, it is always safer to put the lime into the compost heap and thence into the garden. There is danger in using too much lime, for it makes other materials unavailable. Even in the compost heap, lime is applied very sparingly. It might be worth noting here that if garden soil has a good organic matter content, it does not matter so much whether the soil is acid or not. With good compost, one can often grow acid-loving plants in relatively "sweet" soil.

### 8. Why Make a Compost Pile? Why Not Just Dig Each Day's Table Scraps Directly ino the Garden Soil?

Making a compost pile of your table scraps and other organic refuse is preferable, and much safer for the following reasons:

1. The compost pile is a neater place to conceal these wastes.

2. In the compost pile, the wastes can be protected from marauders, rats, mice, dogs, and birds.

3. The compost pile makes a specific place to deposit all scraps and garden trash so that nothing is wasted.

4. By carefully constructing the compost of all kinds of wastes, it is possible to determine exactly how much of each substances goes into the heap. One can thus increase one trace element in the soil by adding materials rich in that substance.

The practice of digging table scraps directly into the soil has several disadvantages:

1. If scraps carry disease, the disease is thus spread all over the neighborhood.

2. In cold weather or in infertile soil, the scraps are not digested by the soil, but remain intact.

3. Undigested trash attracts dogs, rodents, and other scavengers.

4. A garden littered with kitchen scraps is unattractive. Even

the compost pile must be carefully constructed and kept in tidy shape. We were once embarrassed to have visitors inquire if we were raising mushrooms: a large number of eggshells on their way to the compost had fallen rounded side up, so they looked like a fine crop of button mushrooms — right out under the open sky!

### 9. What About Mulching?

1. In a dry season, mulch conserves moisture. A stone mulch is excellent.

2. Mulch discourages weeds and makes weeding easier if any weeds do grow.

3. Some mulch materials, such as buckwheat hulls, make an attractive ground cover.

Mulching is disadvantageous for the following reasons:

1. In a wet season, mulch may allow mildew and moulds to grow on the ground surface thus causing plant stems to rot.

2. If mulch comes too close to garden plants they may grow thin and spindly.

3. A mulch in the orchard harbors and protects field mice which then can easily girdle and kill the young fruit trees.

4. Mulch of hay or straw may sow more seed of that hay or straw.

5. A mulch of hay or straw is hard to distribute aound the plants as they grow in the garden.

6. If one purchases a mulch like buckwheat hulls, it is very expensive.

### 10. How Should we Preserve the Surplus: By Dehydration, Canning, Freezing, or in the Cold Cellar?

Recent studies in chromotography show that dehydration preserves some values in fresh vegetables even better than freezing or canning. For herbs and vegetables chopped very fine, it is possible to dehydrate in small quantities in an electric oven set at "Warm." It should not go over 120°F. and should not continue after the moisture is dried out. Herbs dried in this way retain their green color and, of course, their flavor. When the leaf crumbles, it has dried long enough.

Canning preserves the least of the food values of fresh vegetables and fruits, but has other advantages in readiness to serve on the table. Canning is probably the best way to preserve tomatoes, either whole or in juice, although they may be frozen, contrary to general advice. It is also possible to freeze tomato juice after it has been pressed out. Fruit juice may be frozen directly or it may be pressed out, bottled and pasteurized at a low heat for half an hour. These technical processes should be learned from a government bulletin or from a good cook book, because it is very disappointing to find one's whole harvest of tomatoes spoiled because they were not heated long enough, for instance. This has happened to more than one ardent experimenter!

It is our rule to preserve as many things as possible in the cold cellar to save the labor of freezing and canning. Apples, turnips, beets, carrots, celery, Brussels sprouts, Jerusalem artichokes, potatoes keep well if harvested when they are in good condition. Squash and onions need a slightly warmer place for storage. For further information on storage and preservation see the section on HARVESTING, COOKING AND PRESERVING.

### 11. Why Go to All the Bother of Raising Vegetables When Frozen Ones Are so Good and so Easy to Buy?

One has only to taste fresh vegetables brought in directly from the garden to know how much better they are; and if one freezes one's own, they are still more flavorful than those preserved commercially on a very large scale. However, there are other considerations:

1. Commercially grown crops are usually treated with insecticides which may leave slight residues. If one has concern about this factor in our modern civilization, he can avoid toxic spray residues by raising his own produce.

2. But still more important to the human being is the actual experience of cooperating with soil and sun and air and growth forces to produce something to feed himself out of the earth itself. One doesn't have to explain this to gardeners, and perhaps non-gardeners will never really understand. But the personal attention and nurture adds something intangible which is missing in crops grown on large scale. In recent publicity from Russia the observation has been made by Mr.

Khrushchev that the communal farms are not producing enough, that the small farm units operated by tenant farmers for their own use are producing a far larger percentage of food per unit of space. It has been our experience that food, produced in small quantities by growers with real concern for their creative work, has superior nourishing qualities for both animal and man.

## 12. What Is the Difference Between Bio-Dynamics and Organic Gardening?

Bio-Dynamics is one kind of Organic Gardening, but it is much more than this. Bio-Dynamics is based on the teaching of Rudolf Steiner, who came from peasant stock in Austria in the mid-19th century. He grew up in a small community where he observed the farming customs in use. In later life, when he became a teacher with a tremendous following, he explained many agricultural practices, which were adopted by groups of farmers in Europe and the British Isles. Through the laboratories at the Goetheanum in Switzerland which was founded by Dr. Steiner, these agricultural practices have been tested hundreds of times to prove their soundness. The Biochemical Laboratory in Spring Valley, New York under the direction of the late Dr. E. E. Pfeiffer, a student of Dr. Steiner, has continued the work in agriculture, adding further research on nutrition and quality in foods. Other laboratories in the United States, for instance the facilities of the International Harvester Laboratory, have been employed as a check to make sure there was no bias in the tests. Time after time, Bio-Dynamic agricultural practices have stood up against other less scientific and exacting practices. One thing cannot be emphasized too frequently: for the best results one should convert a whole farm or a whole homestead to Bio-Dynamics. One who uses only two or three of the Bio-Dynamic practices is by no means a Bio-Dynamic farmer. This method is more challenging, takes more study and a much deeper adherence to the correct procedures than other methods. If the criticism is sometimes made that certain Bio-Dynamic practices do not always work, it may well be that they do not work because one has not looked deeply enough into the many interrelationships involved in these processes. With this method there should be no compromise, and in the long run, if the method is followed absolutely and faithfully, the results are most satisfying.

## 13. What Herbs Are Best for Beginners?

Raising herbs is a most enjoyable part of gardening; herbs do not require more than a good fertile soil with adequate compost. They are not troubled by many plant pests, and most herbs are not difficult to grow. They add delicious flavors and scents to the garden and kitchen, as well as a measure of protection to the whole garden from some insects (See section on COMPANION PLANTS.) Until one has experience, it is well to begin with a few herbs so as to learn their culture and uses thoroughly. Chives is already familiar to most people. Many backyard gardeners already have mint of one kind or another, or perhaps catnip growing in their yards. Some easy herbs to add gradually are thyme, oregano, and winter savory —— all perennials. Sage is a biennial in some climates, a perennial in others. One of our most practical is Welsh onion which is perennial and very easy to grow, insuring a plentiful supply of salad onions as soon as the snow melts off the tops in earliest spring, until the hard killing frosts in late fall.

In a Bio-Dynamic garden with raised beds, the end of each bed contains a different herb and the gardener has ample opportunity to study each herb as it passes through the seasons in its relationship with its companion plants. It is a joy to see and sniff these very different, aromatic plants which create such a fragrant atmosphere in the vegetable garden. Dried for the winter, these herbs continue their benevolence for the household in savory seasonings, herb teas, moth-proofing for woolens, and even as an ingredient in cough lozenges. As one's experience increases, it is possible to add more herbs of more complicated habit, like rosemary which has to be brought indoors every winter. A good herb book becomes necessary at this point, but there are many such books of great charm, containing reliable information and intriguing recipes for the herb enthusiast.